meerkat selling

meerkat selling™

Be the Best in Big-Ticket Retail Selling

NICK DRAKE-KNIGHT

pd

PIP
POLLINGER IN PRINT

Pollinger Limited
9 Staple Inn
Holborn
LONDON
WC1V 7QH

www.pollingerltd.com

First published by Pollinger in Print 2008

A CIP catalogue record is available from the British Library

ISBN 978-1-905665-70-9

Designed and set by seagulls.net
Cover design by Gary Jarvis
Cover photograph by Peter Malsbury/iStockPhoto.com
Illustrations by Rupert Besley

Printed and bound in Great Briatin by Lightning Source

Dedicated to Rob, Mart, George and Rosie

contents

ACKNOWLEDGEMENTS

I've met thousands of salespeople either in person, or 'on film' in video mystery shopping recordings. I've been very lucky to have the opportunity to study them in their natural habitats.

To all the *Meerkats, Pre-Judgers, Ickbah Advisers, Desk Controllers, Buying Doctors, Feature Dumpers and Grapeshotters, Brochure Givers, Seed Planters, Order Takers, Convincers, Floppies* and *True Professionals*, thank you for offering such a rich pool of material to study.

My thanks also to Mike Dalloz for his kind and generous Foreword, to Marie Shields for her editing and proofreading excellence, to the fabulous team at Pollinger for their encouragement and good humour, and to Rupert Besley for his intuitive and good fun illustrations.

Nick Drake-Knight
Cliff Cottage, 2008

ICKBAH

about the author

Nick Drake-Knight has been a business change consultant and speaker for more than 20 years. In the 1990s, he developed his consulting skills in Europe and the former Soviet Union, before returning to work in the UK as a senior business adviser for the Department of Trade and Industry funded Business Link network, with a special interest in sales process development.

Nick is a board director of the UK's leading mystery shopping company, Performance in People Ltd., providing sales advice, consultancy and training to many of the UK's (and the world's) top retail and automotive brands.

NDK Group (www.ndk-group.com) is Nick's personal consulting business, providing the platform for his public speaking interests and the source of his popular books.

He is a professionally qualified clinical hypnotherapist (MBSCH, Dhyp) and maintains a small number of private patients. He was trained by NLP co-creator Dr. Richard Bandler to become a Master Practitioner of Neuro-Linguistic Programming and studied extensively as a student with Dr. John Grinder (co-creator of NLP), with fellow change masters Dr.

Frank Farrelly and Dr. Stephen Gilligan, and at the London College of Clinical Hypnosis.

He is an authority on the use of video footage and telephone audio files to train and coach effective sales techniques. He has helped many global brand names to implement his unique Continue & Begin™ coaching model to sustain new sales processes long after the excitement of a training event has faded. The model creates behavioural shifts in employees – quickly.

Nick speaks regularly at national conferences and corporate staff development events. He can be contacted via www.ndk-group.com or by e-mail to nick@ndk-group.com.

Nick Drake-Knight lives on the Isle of Wight, off the south coast of Britain. He is married, with four adult children. He is, without doubt, the worst surfer in England.

Other books by Nick Drake-Knight and available via www.ndk-group.com include:

BOOMERANG! Coach Your Team To Be The Best And See Customers Come Back Time After Time! 254pp, Pollinger in Print, ISBN 978-1-905665-51-8

SALES HYPNOSIS: The Structure and Use of Hypnotic Phenomena and Indirect Suggestion in Sales, 224pp, Hypnotic Business, ISBN 0-9546744-0-5 (co-authored with Fran Osman-Newbury)

foreword

I am delighted to write the foreword for this book. I have had the pleasure of working with Nick Drake-Knight for nearly eight years building our company, Performance in People Ltd, to become one the UK's most successful mystery shopping and retail sales improvement consultancies. We have worked with world-class big-ticket retailers, leading automotive manufacturers and financial services institutions, to evolve their sales processes and create a selling culture of integrity where customers are 'helped to buy'.

We have had the unique opportunity of watching, through video mystery shopping, some of the country's most memorable sales people in action. We have laughed, cheered, squirmed, despaired and on many occasions been quite simply speechless in amazement of what we have seen!

Professional selling, when delivered impeccably, is a joy to observe. We have seen master craftsmen at work weaving a 'spell' of sales magic that leads to both the customer and sales professional achieving their ambitions. The magic, of course, is actually a series of carefully crafted behaviours and language patterns of which the sales professional may or may not be consciously aware.

What Nick has delivered so eloquently in this book is the *structure* of magic that makes exceptional sales people 'exceptional'. The book uncovers the behaviours, processes and psychologies behind successful selling and presents them in a practical and deliverable format, so they may be replicated.

I strongly recommend this book to sales professionals and sales managers engaged in big ticket retail selling.

Once you've got the art of selling licked take a look at Nick's popular coaching book *'BOOMERANG! Coach Your Team To Be The Best And See Customers Come Back Time After Time'*, which does an excellent job of explaining how sales organisations can sustain performance excellence over the longer term.

Mike Dalloz
Chairman and Founder
Performance in People Ltd.
www.performanceinpeople.co.uk

author's note

Not many business consultants get to work with some of the world's leading big-ticket retailers. Fewer still have the opportunity to shape the way those retail giants sell their goods and services to consumers.

In recent years my colleagues and I have been at the centre of thinking about how the sales processes of big-ticket retailers should be delivered and managed. As part of the internal development team of these huge retail organisations I have been able to steer corporate decision makers towards an ethical sales process model I believe in with a burning passion.

Of course, big-ticket retail businesses want ethics, but they also want sales!

The word 'ethical' is important in professional selling. My background in personal change work has helped me think about the sales process from the perspective of the customer, in a manner similar to a therapist considering the needs of a new patient. A patient has come for help. She has taken time from her busy schedule to seek guidance and a 'solution' to the problem that is troubling her. The same model of thought is happening in the mind of a customer visiting a big-ticket retailer.

The parallels with therapeutic counselling are consistent. This similarity in relationship is what Gregory Bateson, the great thinker and father of cybernetics, called a 'pattern which connects'.

The (potential) customer is seeking a solution to a problem. It might be the style of kitchen she has 'hallucinated' for her new home, a furniture suite, a new mobile phone, the holiday she would like, or a new car she is considering. In each case a mild inner turmoil disturbs the customer. It is the task of the true sales professional to help her to think through her options and find a solution that helps her to 'move towards pleasure' or 'move away from pain', whichever is the predominant driving force causing her to seek help.

It is with this benevolent and ethical mind-set that the True Professional can operate with integrity, and as a consequence achieve sales performances far beyond the capabilities of a mere salesperson.

This book describes the sales model I have introduced to some of the UK's most successful big-ticket retailers. The model varies slightly from retailer to retailer to suit industry environments, although the same fundamental five-step framework applies. It is the mind-set of 'understanding and helping' that is the common denominator in the sales teams of these organisations, and which sets them apart as professional and ethical retailers.

What is rather different about the sales process described in this book is the emphasis on indirect suggestion, described in detail in Step 4. I have introduced the idea of indirect suggestions to a number of class-leading retailers. Those who use them as a core part of their selling model report remarkable success.

That's because the more their people use indirect suggestions the more they improve their sales performance. Of course, I don't know which parts of this book will be most useful to you and your colleagues, because only you can decide which elements add the greatest value.

Enjoy the read and you will discover in the very near future, and to your delight, that you have mysteriously begun to use some of these techniques, without even knowing it.

Nick Drake-Knight
Cliff Cottage, 2008

how to use
this book

Meerkat Selling is a learning resource. It provides learning and development for sales professionals at a number of levels. The book is designed to help develop the sales capabilities of individuals, teams and organisations through a range of applications:

- as a reference point for big-ticket retail sales managers to use in the development of sales infrastructures and sales processes
- as a training tool for sales managers to use with sales teams and individual sales professionals (development activities and specific tips are provided at the end of each chapter)
- as a learning resource for customer-facing sales professionals in big-ticket retail environments

Meerkat Selling does not aspire to cover *every* advanced sales technique available to big-ticket retail sales professionals. To do so would require a far lengthier book than this. No, what you have here is a well-proven sales process, with tips and techniques to help, in an easy to absorb five-step format. The purpose of the book is to be user-friendly and that means the learning contained within it should be digestible and *useable*.

If you are experienced in big-ticket retail selling, you may already apply the skills described within this book consistently (note it says 'apply' not 'know'). For you, *Meerkat Selling* will be a useful refresher. If you are relatively inexperienced in big-ticket retail selling, or you are simply curious, you may discover something useful to you in your professional sales role.

Meerkat Selling is presented in three parts:

- **Part A – Sales Management Considerations** (a short introductory section) explores management issues around the development and maintenance of sales process and skills. Prime benefactors of this part of the book will be sales managers.
- **Part B – Professional Selling: Steps 1 to 5** (the main body of the book) presents sales process and sales behaviour knowledge that, with practice, can be turned into skills. Prime benefactors of this part of this part of the book will be sales professionals, either recently entered into the profession or already established and looking to refresh their skill sets. With dedication, and with practise, you can become a True Professional.

  Meerkat Selling presents well-proven sales techniques in short sharp learning chunks. Chunking aids your ability to absorb the underpinning knowledge contained within the book and to rapidly turn knowledge into skilled behaviour. There are no frills, just the essentials.

- **Part C – Taking Action** encourages the sales professional to recognise that taking action is the only true test of learning, because *knowing what to do is not the same as doing what you know.*

PART A

sales management considerations

1

definition of big-ticket retail

In this book the term 'big-ticket retail' includes a diverse collection of retail commodities and services that we all buy from time to time from high street and retail park outlets. The term includes:

- automotive products, including cars, motorcycles, marine craft and bicycles
- home improvement/DIY/DIFY products such as kitchens, bathrooms, bedrooms, conservatories, flooring, conversions
- furniture items
- premium electronic products, including computer equipment
- entertainment centres, TVs and audio products
- white goods
- upmarket jewellery
- holidays
- leisure experiences

The list is far from exhaustive.

Big-ticket items are often an investment in value or long-term performance; that's why customers are generally discerning and considered when it comes to purchasing them. We know from research that in some big-ticket retail sectors the customer will make three or four visits to competitor outlets before making a buying decision, on occasions returning to an earlier store to make the purchase. Big ticket is rarely an impulse purchase.

True sales professionals are aware of the significance to the prospective customer of the big-ticket product and manage the sales process with due respect for the customer.

2
the model
of excellence

Is sales training sufficient to embed a new sales process?

No. There is much more to do than simply train in a new sales process to customer-facing employees.

And yet many sales directors' aspirations for improved sales performance result in a revised training programme for the sales team, delivered with great gusto across the retail estate. Training does play an important role in sales performance improvement. The challenge for senior managers is to choose the most *effective* training methodology to create improved sales capabilities.

Fortunately, some of the world's leading businesses have a helpful 'success pattern' for sales training. The pattern (almost!) guarantees consistent, high-octane performance, with that all-important criterion, *sustainability*.

I identified the pattern during years of working with class-leading retail, automotive and financial services operators. It seemed that in almost every case, the very best big-ticket sales performers in any given business sector had a framework for developing their salespeople. The framework has a common pattern.

The pattern is what Gregory Bateson, the anthropologist and polymath, called a 'pattern which connects' – because it works equally well in a diverse range of big-ticket sales environments. I call it the *Model of Excellence*. The model relates to three levels of influence:

1. Explicit Standards

World-class sales operators have an explicit set of performance standards that spell out exactly what is expected of their sales teams in the form of a 'sales process'. Salespeople need to know what is expected of them if they are to work to a given standard. A sales process provides structured guidance on *how* to sell.

Once trained in the use of the company's sales process, salespeople are expected to use this explicit standard as the procedural and behavioural model to follow when 'selling'.

This is Level 1 in the Model of Excellence (see diagram).

Having an explicit sales process is a start. It won't guarantee salespeople will follow the expected standards of procedure and behaviour, but it does provide a framework for people to work to. The absence of an explicit sales process is usually an indicator of inconsistency in sales approach across an organisation.

2. Consistency

Ask any senior sales executive or operations director in an organisation and they will tell you that across their national or regional estates there are three common standards of sales performance:

1. Pockets of Excellence

Parts of the business where the sales team are firing on all cylinders and consistently produce top results, irrespective of the market and environment in which they operate.

2. Fields of Mediocrity

Usually the majority of the retail network where sales performance is 'OK', just good enough to avoid major concerns, but certainly far from fulfilling the true potential of the retail outlet.

3. Pits of Despair

Those parts of the business where sales performance is dire.

Top-performing organisations strive for consistency of excellence in all geographic and functional areas of their business.

Effective training can help with this, especially when it is practically (competence) based and aligned with explicit standards of performance – the sales process.

Consistency can be stimulated by *effective* training, which stays with the trainee long after the training session has ended. *Effective* sales training combines underpinning knowledge of an appropriate sales process with a mix of embedding techniques. Embedding techniques might include indirect suggestions, metaphors, stories, analogies, fun activities and games, language activities, humour and even mild teasing.

Sales training has to be *fun* and *intriguing* – trainees learn more when they are relaxed and enjoying themselves. If you can make sales trainees curious about learning, they will want more and more knowledge. And confidence comes from underpinning knowledge about product and sales process. All organisations need their salespeople to be confident.

AIR COVER

Buy-in from the top is essential too. There's nothing more influential than a senior manager or director participating in some front-line training. After all, culture starts at the top, doesn't it? A degree of 'air cover' helps too. When middle-ranking managers know that they have the backing of the top people to release staff for essential training, it makes attendance on training events easier to justify.

But here's the rub: consistency is of limited value if it's temporary. World-class operators know that performance excellence must be delivered day in and day out, long after the latest training initiative has been launched. In some organisations, training is like throwing mud against the wall. Most of the mud slides off the wall immediately. Consistency is Level 2 in the Model of Excellence.

3. Sustainability (Sustain – Ability)

Training is a complete waste of energy and resources unless it is made *sustainable*.

New drives for performance improvement, including the introduction of sales process training, are subject to what I call *parachute training*. When organisations implement change, sometimes employees perceive the new project as the 'latest initiative' and the associated training as being delivered by facilitators or consultants who *parachute in*, deliver the training and are then *helicoptered out*.

Parachute training rarely creates lasting change.

We've all been on training courses that are informative, good fun and even useful! The challenge for most of us is that when we get back to the day job our early enthusiasm gradually wanes as we face up to the realities of the daily grind. The commitment to new behaviours often loses momentum after a period of compliance. Even when the whole team experiences the same learning and development programme the 'stick-ability' of the training can be questionable.

Let's face it: few development activities create sustainable changes in behaviour.

It's not surprising then, that many leading retailers have found sales training frustratingly ineffective as a methodology for improving selling performance.

Key to sustainability (Level 3 of the Model of Excellence) is the development of a local coaching philosophy and skill set that allows front-line managers to keep the plates spinning long after a training event has passed. Sustainability through local coaching and management keeps the momentum up and the training alive!

Training must be supported by local leaders who ensure that trainees get the opportunity, encouragement and coaching to implement and maintain their new skills. Successful sales organisations have retail managers who understand that coaching the sales team is a vital ingredient in creating sustainability.

Every professional manager should be able to coach using a consistent methodology – it's a fundamental management competence.

Fortunately help is at hand. In *BOOMERANG! Coach Your Team To Be The Best And See Customers Come Back Time After Time!* (Pollinger in Print, 2007), I provided an insight into how this can be achieved with elegance.

Implementing the Model of Excellence

The Model of Excellence is now widely employed by big-ticket retailers.

The starting point is the creation of an explicit sales process that people can relate to, that they believe is do-able and that they can incorporate into their daily working lives. Make your sales process simple, meaningful and relevant and then train colleagues to deliver it.

Of course, they'll need the sales aids to do the job, and that might mean resource investment. Combine this with a local coaching capability that supports and encourages people, even when they get it wrong, and you have the building blocks for a sustainable model that will create sales excellence across your organisation.

By creating an internal coaching capability, class-leading retailers ensure that sales excellence is sustained. My guidance to you is to follow in the footsteps of acknowledged class leaders and apply this Model of Excellence to your operations:

1. Decide on your sales process – make it explicit and simple.

2. Create a coaching culture and coaching process within your organisation that *everyone* uses. See *BOOMERANG!* for the most effective coaching model for big-ticket retail.

3. Train your people in the selling skills they need to succeed at their jobs.

4. Maintain post-training sales performance through regular coaching by local managers.

3

the sales engine

Successful big-ticket retail organisations recognise the benefits of developing a sales engine for their retailing teams. A sales engine starts by recognising that a certain number of prospective customers cross over the retail threshold every day and these visitors represent your sales population. This is the 'footfall driver'.

Most retailers invest heavily in marketing to encourage prospective customers to visit the 'shop'. Having attracted them, the job of the sales professional is to convert their interest into a sale.

Sales engine structures vary from business to business, with slightly different formats dependent on the retail sector. For example, some big-ticket retailers work to an appointment system, with customers asked to 'sit' as participants in the design process. Home improvement retailers, including kitchen, bathrooms and bedroom suppliers, are a good example.

In the automotive sector the test drive is an important feature of the process and is hugely influential in encouraging a customer to buy. By converting an enquiry to a test drive the chances of a sale increase significantly.

CONVERSION TO SIT

The key learning point for big-ticket retail sales professionals is the MASSIVE performance increases achievable from relatively small incremental improvements in each stage of the selling process. In many cases, an improvement of as little as 10 percent at each stage will result in a more than 40 percent overall sales increase.

The sales engines described below are simplistic models with only a few stepping stones. Even so, they are fairly typical, with sales drivers that include:

- footfall number
- staff availability/deployment
- engagement/approach
- conversion to 'sit', or test drive
- conversion to order
- average order value

Even with simple sales engines, the impact of incremental improvement across a limited range of sales drivers impacts significantly on sales values.

Sales Engine (automotive – car sales)

		CURRENT PERFORMANCE	10% PERFORMANCE IMPROVEMENT
Sales Pool	Customer footfall	100	100
Customer Engagement	Prospective customers engaged %	80%	88%
	= number of prospective customers	80	88
	Static vehicle demonstration %	75%	82.5%
	= number of static demos	60	72
	Test drive %	50%	55%
	= number of test drives	30	40
Conversion Rate	Conversion rate from test drive to sale	50%	55%
	= number of sales	15	22
AOV – ATV	Average transaction/ order value	£20,000	£22,000
Sales Value	Sales value	£300,000	£484,000
	Performance uplift £		£184,000
	Performance uplift %		61%

Sales Engine (bathrooms)

		CURRENT PERFORMANCE	10% PERFORMANCE IMPROVEMENT
Sales Pool	Customer footfall	1000	1000
Customer Engagement	Sales staff are physically available to engage customers	85%	93.5%
	= number of customers	850	935
	We approach 'x' %	63%	69.3%
	= number of customers	536	648
	Conversion rate to appointment	10%	11%
	= number of apointments	53	71
Conversion Rate	Conversion rate to order	(say) 50%	55%
	= number of orders	26	39
AOV – ATV	Average transaction/ order value	£1750	£1925
Sales Value	Sales Value	£45,500	£75,075
	Performance improvement £		£29,575
	Performance improvement %		65%

Development Activities

- *What is the sales engine for your organisation?*
- *What are the sales drivers?*
- *When will you start measuring your sales engine performance as a regular activity?*
- *What percentage improvement do you want to apply?*
- *What is the impact of an x percent incremental increase across all the drivers in your sales engine?*

4

deployment

ICBA

I continue to be staggered at the lack of correlation between some big-ticket retailers' deployment models and the reality of what happens in-store – because I'm stuffed if I can find a sales adviser when I need one. They're just not there. If they are there, they're often busy with another customer, or just can't be bothered to approach me.

The *ICBA Advisers* (pronounced *ickbah*, as in *'I can't be arsed'*) drive me nuts, and so do the *Desk Controllers* – those lazy salespeople who are so busy looking after their paperwork and computer screens that they don't have time for distractions from prospective customers. After all, if it weren't for all those customers on the sales floor they'd be able to get their admin done on time. That's not a deployment issue though, it's an **em**ployment issue.

Footfall patterns are the barometers for deployment planning. Deployment is about fitting your sales resource to the needs of the market place, not the other way round.

I've visited hundreds of stores and showrooms up and down the UK, and I have rarely been approached promptly by a salesperson. I'm sure the implementation of your deployment model is managed superbly and reflects the footfall patterns of your visiting customers. Just check the reality, OK?

DESK CONTROLLER

5

you've got enough prospective customers

The reality for most big-ticket retailers is that more than enough people cross the threshold; it's just that too few are engaged in conversation by the sales team. In fact, footfall is rarely the challenge; it's the conversion of visitors that offers the real opportunity for improvement.

When big-ticket retailers analyse footfall conversion rates, the following ratios are quite common:

- 100 visitors across threshold
- 50 can't see a sales adviser
- 10 can see an adviser, but are not approached
- 40 get approached, but are greeted with an ineffective introduction (e.g. *"Can I help you?"*)

The options for most retailers are simple:

1. Maintain the same poor engagement and conversion ratios, and increase footfall through (expensive) marketing initiatives.
2. Improve engagement and conversion ratios of existing footfall volumes.
3. A combination of the above.

The most cost effective, and sustainable, methodology is to improve the engagement and conversion capability of big-ticket retail outlets. The costs associated with improving these essential components of the sales engine are considerably less than high profile marketing campaigns that have relatively short life spans.

Sustainability is the key, and this is best achieved through a combination of sales process clarity, training to achieve consistency, and a robust mechanism of local coaching (usually supported by video mystery shopping) to keep up the good work long after the training sessions have ended.

So, what has to happen to improve engagement and conversion ratios? The answer lies in the 5-Step Selling Model.

Helping People to Buy

Generally speaking, people do not like to be 'sold' to. Being manipulated or coerced into behaviour is an unpleasant experience for most of us. By contrast, when we have an urge to purchase we really do want a professional to help us buy whatever the product or service is we desire.

HELP NEEDED

Throughout *Meerkat Selling*, the emphasis is on *helping people to buy*. In big-ticket selling, there is a causal connection between prospective customers visiting a big-ticket retail outlet, and their internal thought processes. There is always a *reason* for their visit to your store.

A well-structured sales process helps customers to do what they want to do – to buy the big-ticket product they desire.

6

sales process

A professional sales process provides a road map for successful selling. Assuming that the sales process is an effective one, professional salespeople need only stick to the process to achieve some degree of success. *Not* sticking to a good sales process is almost certain to result in inconsistent performance, even if working 'off-piste' results in moderate achievements.

WORKING OFF-PISTE

Some sales individuals will thrive without a structured approach to their selling style. In the most part however, a guided framework of proven methods is more likely to achieve good results, **consistently**.

Sales processes exist for a number of reasons:

- to aid new starters in learning to sell professionally
- to provide a guidance framework for existing sales professionals
- to create a consistent approach to selling across the business
- to capitalise on sales opportunities
- to ensure a professional presentation of your business by your sales representatives

Most big-ticket retailers have a sales process of some kind. It will vary from sector to sector, and from company to company, but the truth is, there are only so many ways of skinning the sales process cat.

The components of a good sales process include a number of activities that, when categorised, tend to fall into a limited number of behaviours:

1. meeting and greeting customers
2. understanding customers' wants and needs
3. demonstrating products and/or services that meet those wants and needs
4. summarising and recommending a specific solution that meets the wants and needs
5. closing the sale

Some sales processes are shorter, with two or more of the above behaviours combined into one activity. Other sales processes are extended, creating additional steps. The reality is that most organisations have very similar sales processes; it's just the segmentation that varies.

5-Step Selling Model

The 5-Step Selling Model described above is fairly standard in big-ticket retail. The language used for each step may differ, and there will sometimes be an internally devised acronym somewhere in the mix, but essentially this is the most common framework of behaviours forming the sales process. Other descriptions might include:

STEP 1
Meeting and greeting customers
- Approach
- Acknowledge
- Availability
- Building rapport
- Opening the relationship
- Building a relationship
- Positive greeting
- Welcome
- First impressions
- Arrival
- Connect

STEP 2

Understanding needs

- Qualification/qualify
- Question the customer's needs
- Listen
- Obtain
- Identify wants
- Identify needs
- Consult
- Identify customer need
- Understand
- Fact-find

STEP 3

Demonstrating products and/or services

- Explanation
- Show
- Describe
- Match needs
- Meet needs
- Help customer

STEP 4

Summarising and recommending

- Summarise
- Suggest
- Satisfy needs
- Prompt
- Advise
- Deliver

STEP 5

Closing the sale

- Ask for the order
- Close
- Place order
- Invite purchase
- Gain agreement
- Commitment
- Confirmation
- Conclusion
- Consolidate
- Wrap up
- Follow up

Some sales organisations will blend together some of these stages. The most common combination of the five-step model components is to merge Steps 3 and 4, or 4 and 5 as follows:

1. Meet and greet
2. Understand needs
3. **Demonstrate and Recommend**
4. Close

Or,

1. Meet and greet
2. Understand needs
3. Demonstrate
4. **Recommend and Close**

The process is pretty much the same; again, it's just the segmentation of the process components that is presented differently.

7

conscious memory
(7 plus or minus 2)

What we know about the ability of salespeople to absorb and then deliver on a sales process is regulated by the capacity of each individual to consciously recall the steps of the process during a discussion with a prospective customer.

What is significant is the number of pieces of information the salesperson is expected to retain and recall. Chunking into sections, along the lines of the four or five steps described above, is a good starting point. George Miller identified that most people can consciously absorb and retain between five and nine pieces of information at any given time; thus the description '7, plus or minus 2'. The safe bet is to go for no more than five. A sales process that contains more than five component parts is asking for trouble!

There are inevitably a good number of behaviours and subsidiary activities within each of the five steps. Because our minds are adept at chunking information and linking ideas to one another, we can easily remember sets of information within each of these chunks. Each of the five step chunks has a lower logical level of components that form a set of behaviours. For example, Step 2, 'Understand needs', is one of a set of five chunks:

1. Meeting and greeting customers
2. **Understand needs**
3. Demonstrating products and/or services
4. Recommending a specific solution
5. Closing the sale

Within the chunk 'Understand needs' are a series of additional sets of behaviours that professional salespeople utilise. These may include:

2. **Understand needs**
  2.1 Ask good questions
  2.2 Listen actively
  2.3 Understand the customer's Emotional Driver™
  2.4 Determine needs and wants
  2.5 Clarify 'fuzzy language'

As you can see, another five components exist within this lower logical level, or chunk of information. Within each of these chunks may exist another, lower logical level of behaviours or activities that make up each component. A good example here is '2.1 Ask good questions'. This component may be broken down as follows:

2.1 Ask good questions

2.1.1   Ask open questions

2.1.2   Ask 'freedom questions'

2.1.3   Ask probe questions

2.1.4   Ask instant replay questions

2.1.5   Ask closed questions

Each chunk is easy to recall if it is part of a set of information that does not break the '7 plus or minus 2' rule. Each chunk links to a sub-set of smaller chunks, which, if contained within a limited set, are easy to retain and recall.

These are fundamental rules in memory access and a good reason why a sales process should not exceed five steps.

8

monitoring your sales process

The best way to monitor and measure the realities of how your sales process is being delivered in-store is to implement a mystery shopping programme.

Mystery shopping comes in range of formats:

- video mystery shopping (hidden camera)
- 'report only' mystery shopping (no recording equipment)
- telephone mystery shopping
- e-mail mystery shopping

Each format has its place and can be used really effectively to monitor and measure sales behaviours and process compliance.

Most national big-ticket retailers commission a report-only mystery shop programme, usually on a monthly basis. Report-only is great for identifying trends in behaviour and the parts of the sales process being fully complied with, and those being addressed with less dedication by sales staff.

However, as a personal learning and development tool it is less effective.

By far the most productive mystery shopping programme, in terms of learning and development, is the covert video format.

Video mystery shopping highlights the non-verbal elements of human communication, including tone of voice, facial expressions, eye movement and breathing patterns, as well as minor and major motor movements. The communication process, including the dialogue between sales adviser and customer, is revealed in all its glory – or lack of it.

The mystery shop is verifiable; that is, it can be referred to for the purposes of coaching an individual and (with the permission of the featured salesperson) her colleagues in her sales team. Video mystery shopping is a profoundly powerful resource for helping people to recognise the aspects of the sales process in which they are clearly proficient, and to highlight those areas where they could be *even better.*

BOOMERANG! explains in detail how video mystery shopping can be used to create phenomenal increases in sales performance. World-class big-ticket retail organisations understand the influence of video mystery shopping.

Below is a typical video mystery shopping evaluation report for the big-ticket division of a home improvement chain. Notice how the report reflects key parts of the sales process.

Video mystery shop evaluation report

(Big-Ticket Home Improvement)

Step 1 Meet and Greet

1. **Did the salesperson acknowledge the customer within 1 minute of customer entering the show-room?** Acknowledgement can be a nod, a *"Hello"* or *"I'll be with you in a minute"* comment, or similar.

   Y ☐ N ☐

2. **Did the salesperson approach the customer with a smile within 3 minutes of customer entering the showroom?** Self explanatory Y ☐ N ☐

3. **Did the salesperson build rapport with the customer?** The salesperson must attempt to build rapport with the customer through personal introduction, a truism or open question. Y ☐ N ☐

4. **Did the salesperson ask what research the customer had already conducted?** The salesperson must identify what background research the customer has already undertaken in searching for a new product. Y ☐ N ☐

Step 2 Qualify Requirements

5. **Did the salesperson ask open questions and actively**

listen to establish the customer's requirements? The salesperson must ask at least two open questions to establish the customer's needs. He or she must demonstrate active listening by repeating the understanding of these needs. Y ❑ N ❑

6. **Did the salesperson attempt to uncover the customer's Emotional Drivers? (underlying reason for purchase)** The salesperson must *attempt* to uncover the customer's Emotional Driver. This is the emotional reason for the customer's potential purchase. Emotional Drivers are separate from the practical needs the purchase will have to satisfy. Y ❑ N ❑

7. **Did the salesperson ask for any 'must haves'?** The salesperson must ask the customer for any essential features or benefits of the product. Y ❑ N ❑

8. **Did the salesperson ask for any 'constraints'?** The salesperson must ask the customer for any constraints regarding the product or project. Y ❑ N ❑

9. **Did the salesperson ask for the customer's planned *investment* in the product or project?** The salesperson must ask the customer about the *investment* he or she plans to make – NOT 'budget'. The investment may be a total price or a monthly figure. Y ❑ N ❑

10. **Did the salesperson mention finance and services available?** Self-explanatory Y ❑ N ❑

11. **Did the salesperson establish the time scales for the purchase?** Self-explanatory   Y ☐ N ☐

12. **Did the salesperson deepen rapport by using clean language?** The salesperson must use the customer's own words and phrases *at least twice* during the discussion.

    Y ☐ N ☐

Step 3 Demonstrate

13. **Did the salesperson give a full demonstration of the product, explaining the features and benefits?** Self-explanatory   Y ☐ N ☐

14. **Did the salesperson link features and benefits back to the customer's requirements?** The salesperson must link product and service features and benefits back to the customer's stated requirements. Just listing features ('feature dumping') will not score.   Y ☐ N ☐

15. **Did the salesperson offer good-better-best alternatives?** The salesperson must present three alternative levels of quality as choices for the customer.

    Y ☐ N ☐

16. **Did the salesperson use *amplification* to reinforce positive comments from the customer?** The salesperson must confirm any positive customer comments

regarding the product and service offer by repeating back *at least one* agreement on the customer's positive comments and 'amplifying' them back by adding 'very', 'really', or similar words, e.g. *"Yes, it is really handy."*

Y ☐ N ☐

17. **Did the salesperson attempt a trial close during the demonstration phase?** The salesperson must test the appropriateness of the demonstration by asking trial close questions such as *"Is that the kind of thing you are looking for/interested in?"* or *"Would that be of interest to you?"* or *"Is that what you are after?"* or similar.

Y ☐ N ☐

Step 4 Summarise and Recommend

18. **Did the salesperson summarise the sales process 'so far' and then recommend a specific product?** The salesperson must summarise by saying, *"Based on what you've told me ..."* or similar. Y ☐ N ☐

19. **Did the salesperson make a clear recommendation of the best solution?** The salesperson must make a concise recommendation. This may include products and services. Y ☐ N ☐

20. **Did the salesperson tie recommended products and services to the customer's Emotional Driver?** The salesperson must tie the recommended products and services back to the customer's Emotional Driver or

stated requirements. Failure to <u>attempt</u> to uncover the customer's Emotional Drivers (Q6) will mean no score for this question.   Y ☐ N ☐

Step 5 Close and Consolidate

21. Did the salesperson use the 'yes set' summary? The salesperson must ask the customer a series of questions that create a 'yes set' of answers.   Y ☐ N ☐

22. Did the salesperson ask for the order? The salesperson must make a clear closed question request to place the order, such as *"Shall I place the order for you?"* or *"Would you like me to arrange delivery for you?"* or *"Shall we go with that one?"* or similar.   Y ☐ N ☐

23. Did the salesperson attempt to link sell? The salesperson must make attempt to link sell associated products or services related to the main sale item, to add value for the customer.   Y ☐ N ☐

24. Did the salesperson attempt to consolidate? The salesperson must attempt to consolidate. This may be to agree the next steps with the customer, to check the order/plan, to explain the after-sales process or discuss delivery details.   Y ☐ N ☐

25. <u>If the customer declines to place the order today,</u> did the salesperson ask the specific reason for the decline? The salesperson must ask the reason for the decline to purchase and make a written record for possible 'follow up'.   Y ☐ N ☐

26. <u>**If the customer declines to place the order today,**</u>
did the salesperson attempt to secure customer
details, including name, and contact number,
address or email address. Self-explanatory

Y ☐ N ☐

Step 6 Follow-up

27. <u>**If the customer declined to place the order on the**</u>
<u>**day,**</u> **did the salesperson follow up within three**
days? The salesperson must follow up within three days
to explore customer progress. Failure to <u>attempt</u> to
secure customer details (Q26) will mean no score for
this question.   Y ☐ N ☐

A Note for Marketing Directors and Brand Experience Managers

Here's a thought: the manner in which your products and services are sold impacts hugely on your brand. A professional sales process, delivered consistently, reflects positively on your brand.

Video mystery shopping is a fabulous way to measure the reality of how your sales process is actually being delivered, as opposed to how you think it is being delivered.

PART B

professional selling
(steps 1 to 5)

9

step 1
meet and greet

Meerkatting

MEERKATS

Meerkatting is a defining feature of the big-ticket retail superstar.

Top performers recognise the value of footfall and just like meerkats, they keep their eyes peeled for movement on the horizon. Customers entering a store or dealership are there for a reason – they are interested in making a purchase. This doesn't mean that they are necessarily committed to making a purchase, but it does mean they are a warm lead – otherwise they wouldn't have come in to look around!

Warm leads are gold dust. Retailers and automotive manufacturers spend millions on marketing campaigns to position their brands and create interest, but ultimately the aim is to encourage prospects to visit product distribution points. Meerkatting means scanning your store or dealership, and the area immediately outside too, for signs of interest from prospective customers.

The top sales stars know the value of meerkating and keep on their toes at all times, ready to move when a customer needs help.

Development Activities
- *Practise meerkating for one full week and notice the difference in your customer engagement activity levels.*

Pre-Judging

We often pre-judge people when we first meet them. You will have done this on occasions – we all have. The challenge comes when we pre-judge prospective customers. We pre-judge people by our own prejudices of how people look, how people speak, and how they behave. Some features of prospective customers that influence salespeople can include the customer's:

- age
- gender
- dress/clothing
- grooming – smart or scruffy
- accent or dialect
- ethnicity

- mannerisms
- weight, complexion, apparent health

Salespeople are well known for making a rapid assessment of a prospective customer as being a likely buyer, or a time waster or a dreamer.

Pre-judging a prospective customer is a risky thing to do! Today there are no rules about how people 'should be'. Big-ticket purchases are made by the most surprising people – people who d*on't look like they could afford it.*

When you are meerkatting, make sure you are open-minded about everyone who visits your showroom.

Acknowledgement, Approach and Engagement

Meerkatting increases the chances of spotting a prospective customer. Next up we need to communicate with our visitor!

Acknowledgement, approach and engagement are the three stages of movement from initial awareness of a visitor through to engaging in conversation that encourages a *visitor* to move from being a *prospect* to becoming a *customer.*

Acknowledgement can be something as simple as a nod, a raised eyebrow, or a quick *"Hello"*. It might include a little more, with something like *"Hi, I'll be with you in moment,"* - useful if you are engaged with another customer at the time.

Approach is about finding the right timing to physically move towards a prospective customer. A number of big-ticket retailers like their sales professionals to allow customers time to browse before approaching. There is nothing worse than being pounced on as soon as you enter a store or dealership. The challenge, of course, is to find the balance between immediate pouncing and the dangers of leaving a customer too long. This is why the acknowledgement phase is so crucial. Customers need to know that they have been noticed and that *you* are ready to engage in conversation when *they* are ready to do so. Most customers will give off small non-verbal signs that suggest they are ready for some assistance.

These 'help needed' messages are often conveyed by their facial expressions, by looking around, by shifting their weight from one foot to the other, or by rubbing their faces with their hands.

The key to approaching is to be as non-threatening as possible. Open arms, a big smile and smart appearance are all that is required. You already know how to be friendly.

Engagement is the process of actually talking to a prospective customer. We will cover this is in more detail in Truisms and Bridging Questions.

Research conducted in the UK by one major big-ticket retailer identified that in their stores, out of every 10 visitors, six could not find a sales employee available to consult, three could see a sales consultant but were not approached, and only one (10 percent!) was acknowledged, approached and engaged in conversation. What a waste!

Think of all the sales opportunities lost through low levels of engagement. Of course, some of the limitations in staff availability are due to deployment issues – that is, the management of people resources. Other reasons include poor staff training, poor leadership and occasional bouts of ICBA *(Ickbah)*.

It is the local manager's job to instil energy and passion into the sales team, and for the salespeople themselves to have the self-motivation to succeed. Acknowledgement, Approach and Engagement are fundamentals of good sales practice. Managers have to lead from the front on the sales floor by exhibiting these behaviours themselves.

Development Activities (for sales professionals)

- *Practice acknowledging prospective customers, waiting for signs of 'help needed', and approaching with friendly professionalism.*

Development Activities (for sales managers)

- *Why do some sales staff fail to approach customers as much as you would like them to?*
- *What are the solutions for overcoming the lack of approaches so that your store/dealership can perform even better?*
- *How have you coached your own staff, and how have you been coached to address this challenge?*

One Chance Only

It's cliché time: *"You never get a second chance to create a first impression."*

Initial impressions are created in just a few seconds. In sales this means you have to be quick and get the customer at the right time with a really positive impression of yourself. If the first impression is 'less good' it can take a lot of work to change someone's mind about you. Initial impressions create a reference point for other people, who then look for confirmation that their initial assessment of you was accurate. They look for evidence to support their assessment.

It's not a done deal though. First impressions can be temporary. With some work involving rapport building, even 'less good' first impressions can be turned round – its just that there's no need to put yourself at an unnecessary disadvantage in the first place.

Ask yourself:

- How do I present myself to my visiting customers?
- What do I look like, sound like? (Smell like?)

The professional approach to ensuring a good first impression is simple: be prompt, be bright, look smart, and be genuinely friendly.

Development activities

- *Check out your appearance in the mirror. Are you as smart as you could be? Ask a trusted colleague for a second opinion, or ask him or her to video record you – you may be surprised by what you see!*

Rapport

Rapport is an essential sales skill. Rapport can be described as:

- bonding
- affinity
- empathy
- friendship
- harmony

- understanding
- interrelationship
- being on the same level
- speaking the same language
- singing from the same hymn sheet
- sharing the same world
- being in touch

A key element of professional selling skills is to build rapport with prospective customers so that you have the best chance of a successful sales outcome. Rapport can be demonstrated in shared interests, shared beliefs, shared words, shared tone and shared posture or shared physiology. It's about being friendly.

Eye contact, a smile and a greeting are the very least a customer should expect, and these go some way towards creating rapport with customers. As well as this, there are some skills you can use to develop rapport at a deeper level.

The key to building rapport with a customer is to be as natural as possible. Even people new to selling already know how to be friendly and approachable – it is a social skill we learn from an early age. Rapport-building skills can be enhanced by a few simple techniques, which, if used regularly, quickly become habit.

Verbals and Non-Verbals

When we meet customers for the first time, we give off messages in verbal and non-verbal communication. Verbal communication comes in the form of word content, sentence construction and tone of voice. Non-verbal messages are conveyed by the way we

NON-VERBAL
SIGNS

present our bodies to customers, our facial expressions, eye movements, our posture, our skin tone and our breathing. Some of these non-verbal messages can be actively controlled, but many are unconscious mannerisms or physical traits that we are unaware of. They are driven by how we feel at a given moment.

One of the great benefits of visual mystery shopping (that is, mystery shopping using hidden secret cameras) is the massive impact it has on employees 'featured' in the film.

For years I have been coaching sales staff featured on film. Almost every time the sales professional will make immediate comment on how he or she 'looked' or 'sounded' – commentary on personal presentation and behaviour.

Most people are aware of the significance of non-verbal messaging and the impact it can have on others. In the field of professional selling this is a vital area to get right. Successful sales professionals present themselves as competent and confident in their roles (without being perceived as arrogant), while being respectful and considerate of their customers' needs, wants and emotions.

Key elements of your body language will include:

- gestures
- eye movements
- head and hand movements
- facial expression
- breathing patterns
- direction of gaze
- proximity positioning – how close you stand to people
- orientation (sitting, standing etc.)
- speed of movement
- bodily contact

We know from studies that when a person's words, tone and body language send different messages, it is the body language first and tone second, that score most points in communicating meaning and intent. Put simply, you can say whatever welcoming introductory comments you like, but if the tone you use is not equally welcoming, or your facial expressions and body movement suggest otherwise, you will give off contrary messages to the prospective customer. The customer will believe your non-verbal message more than the words you have spoken.

Congruency

Research indicates that congruency of verbal and non-verbal communication is important. That is to say, giving off messages with the spoken word must be mirrored by non-verbal messages if a customer is to believe the friendliness of the salesperson is genuine. It's no good using *words* that are friendly and helpful if the manner in which words are said do not give off the same 'vibe'.

It seems that when a salesperson's verbal and non-verbal communication present contradictory messages, there is a hierarchy of belief in the mind of the customer. In effect, tone is more influential than the words, and body language more influential than tone.

In practice this means, with regard to, say friendliness:

- *Verbal message* of friendliness combined with a *tone message* that is <u>unfriendly</u>
  = Tone message is believed
- Friendly *verbal message* <u>and</u> friendly *tone message* combined with a *non-verbal (body language)* message that is <u>unfriendly</u>
  = Non-verbal (body language) message is believed

The same equation applies to whatever message is being assessed by the customer, e.g. friendliness, knowledge about product, confidence, genuineness, honesty, solution-focused rather than selling-focused.

During the early 1970s Albert Mehrabian conducted extensive research into the conflicting messages we sometimes transmit during the communication process. *Silent Messages* is the book to read for a more detailed understanding of this fascinating subject.

Development Activity

- *Get yourself filmed practising your sales process with a colleague. Check out the words you use, the tone with which you use them, and how you use your body. Do they all give the same message? Are they 'congruent'?*

- *Is the message one you would like to receive as a prospective big-ticket customer?*

The Confidence Pyramid

Whenever I've worked with sales professionals, one of their primary drivers to success has been confidence. Almost without exception, successful salespeople report that personal confidence plays a key role in their ability to perform.

But how can an aspiring True Professional achieve confidence in a sales role?

Confidence is a function of knowledge and experience. The diagram below illustrates exactly how knowledge and experience contribute to personal confidence. And don't just take my word for it. Every sales professional I've ever met agrees with this model, because it is a true reflection of how confidence is achieved.

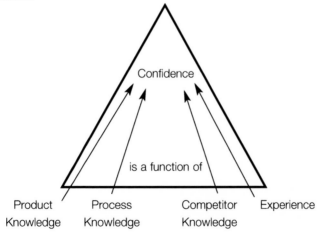

This is excellent news, because with a degree of personal application most of the confidence drivers can be learned, or gained through time.

What is does mean though, is that you will need to:

- know your product (inside out!)
- know your offer – including prices, additional services, delivery, etc.
- know all about competitor products and services – what's good about them, and what's 'less good'
- know your sales process (this book might help!)
- know what has worked, and not worked, in the past

Confidence comes when you have good knowledge of your product or service range and your competitor's products, good knowledge of your sales process and customer service processes, and a measure of experience. When you are genuinely confident you'll find appropriate non-verbal behaviour will come naturally.

Development activities

- *Consider the types of body language you might expect to notice in relation to projecting an image of confidence. Think in particular about the meet and greet situation and engaging customers in conversation.*
- *What is your product knowledge like?*
- *What is your knowledge of your sales process and customer service processes?*
- *Are there specific areas of your job role that you can focus on to gain more experience?*
- *Copy the table below and plot your thoughts on the indicators of confidence:*

Confidence in Non-verbal Communication

	Communicating Confidence	Communicating Lack of Confidence
Posture, Arms, Hands	Relaxed, arms by side, open palms, weight on both feet	Behind desk or computer barrier, folded arms, slumped, hands in pockets, head and shoulders lowered
Eyes		
Face		
Voice		
Movement, Walking		

People Buy From People
(But not if they don't like the salesperson)

My chum Richard is a mad keen motorcyclist. He loves the thrill of full-on supersports machines that accelerate so fast they leave your insides back at the traffic lights.

He's owned all sorts of manufacturers' bikes and raves about them all. Every three or four years he will spend around £9,000 on a new machine. But there's one brand of motorcycle he won't buy. It's not because the bikes are poor – far from it, he knows the XXX brand is fantastic and the machines are at the cutting edge of engineering design.

No, he won't buy this particular brand because some years ago Adam, the owner of the local XXX motorcycle dealership, made disparaging remarks about Richard's then new motorbike (a different brand of machine). Richard thinks Adam is an arse.

Incidentally, criticising someone's previous buying decisions is a classic sales mistake. It implies the salesperson thinks the customer is an idiot – not exactly a successful rapport building strategy.

Richard knows that he could buy a XXX brand of machine from another dealership, but that would mean servicing locally and he would almost certainly have to talk to Adam at some stage, and pay him servicing costs that inevitably provide a profit for Adam.

An alternative is to buy this brand of motorcycle from a non-local dealer and have it serviced non-locally, but that would be irksome.

No, Richard has decided that he will buy his motorcycles from anywhere other than the local dealership. He'd rather slit his eyeballs with a razor than buy a motorcycle from Adam.

Because Adam is an arse.

I like motorbikes too; I have owned a few different manufacturing brands over the years. Richard is my friend, and I wouldn't dream of buying a motorcycle from the local dealership. Rich would never speak to me again.

People buy from people.

Act As If

In big-ticket retail selling, it is clearly important that a salesperson builds rapport with prospective customers through effective communication. But how can this be done? It seems a challenging task for a new salesperson to master rapport. One really helpful technique is to 'act as if'.

The principle of *Act As If* is a great way of building rapport with customers. Put simply, all you need to do is 'act as if' you are friendly and approachable.

It seems that simply acting 'as if' we are friendly and helpful causes our bodies and voice to operate in a friendly and helpful way – we don't need to concentrate on the mechanics of our verbal and non-verbal mannerisms, they simply slot into place naturally as a result of acting in that way. This is great news for people learning for the first time how to behave with customers, because they are already highly skilled and experienced!

There are questions to ask yourself if you want to 'act as if' you are warm, friendly, approachable and engaging:

1. How does someone who is warm and friendly approach customers?

2. What does someone who is warm and friendly say, as they approach a customer?

3. What tonality does someone who is warm and friendly use, as they speak to customers?

4. How does someone who is warm and friendly use their body and body language, as they speak to customers?

These and similar questions provide the basis for deciding how we would operate if we were to Act As If we really are a successful at approaching customers in a friendly and helpful way. If we Act As If, then we become.

What's great about acting as if you are really friendly is that you don't need to learn masses of 'schmoozing' techniques for engaging the customer in an introductory conversation to get them to open up. And it's not necessary to have a list of pre-prepared 'intro-phrases' either. Simply Act As If you are friendly and you will be – you already know how to do it.

Development Activity

- *What are the behaviours you need to develop?*
- *How would you 'Act As If' using the questions above?*

Clean Language

Clean Language is a rapport building technique that employs a simple principle: if I use the same words as you, then we have a greater possibility of creating a rapid rapport based on mutual use of language. The less we try to paraphrase or adapt the language used by other people into our own preferred language, and the more we use *their* chosen words and sentence construction, the more likely it is that our fellow communicators will feel a sense of understanding and empathy from us.

This has proven to be a powerful rapport building technique. Where possible, key words from the speaker's language patterns are repeated back by the rapport builder. The skill is in identifying which words to repeat back and when, in order for the other person to feel that the process is a natural activity rather than a conscious, contrived, 'technique'.

At any time during the sales experience, you have the opportunity to 'use the words the customer uses' in order to confirm and demonstrate that you do understand what she is saying. This maximises rapport, and sales!

> *Customer:* "I've got £5,000 to spend and not a penny more. So keep that in mind."
> *Sales Adviser:* "OK, I'll keep that in mind – £5,000. If we make the most of the offers, I could even give you a few pennies back, how would that be?"

> *Customer:* "I want a leather interior, with a leather steering wheel and a leather gear-stick knob."
> *Sales Adviser:* "Have a look at this leather interior, it's got a leather steering wheel and I can get you a leather gear-stick knob."

> *Customer:* "I really want it to look like real wood and it must be easy to clean."
> *Sales Adviser:* "OK, let me show you the real wood finishes and I can show you how easy it is to clean."

> *Sales Adviser:* "What you said earlier was 'hard wearing' and you said you were prepared to pay a bit extra for something that would last longer."
> *Customer:* "Yes, I did say that."
> *Sales Adviser:* "Now this one is one you can pay a bit extra for, compared to the others, and it's so hard wearing, just like you wanted … "

You get the idea?

Clean Language is hugely powerful if delivered in a natural style. We know that we can quietly echo some key words, often mid-way through a speaker's delivery, perhaps with a nodding head that gives the impression of true, empathetic understanding. We can ask questions of customers, using their already-spoken words and phrases, to clarify our understanding of their thoughts and at the same time confirming to the customer that we have listened – after all, we must have listened, because we are using their words!

Clean Language emphasises to the customer that we have listened and that we 'speak the same language'. It's a great rapport building technique.

Development Activity

- *Practise clean language with a colleague 'in the know' and get feedback on how elegant and natural you were.*
- *Practise clean language with customers from now on. From now on? That's right, from now on.*

Truisms

Approaching a prospective customer to initiate discussion and begin the sales process is a critical moment. Some people dislike approaching customers and are concerned about being rejected.

We know that asking, *"Can I help you?"* or *"Are you OK there?"* actually encourages rejection, and so are best avoided.

Using *truisms* is a great way to approach a customer in a gentle manner that avoids tension or resistance and quickly builds up trust. In fact, hypnotists use truisms to induce trance in their patients!

To use truisms with customers, you merely have to notice where they are and what they're doing.

A truism is a statement of obvious truth, a statement that the recipient must accept. One successful sales manager refers to truisms as, *"A statement of the bleeding obvious!"* A truism is undeniable and is the first step towards developing a natural 'non-salesy' conversation.

Here are a few simple examples of sales truisms:

"I see you are looking at the walk-in shower."

"It can be difficult to decide sometimes."

"This is the diesel engine version."

"There are so many holidays to choose from."

"It's wet outside today."

"I've noticed – you've been looking at the Dolomite range."

"Make yourself comfortable, choosing the right suite is important."

"Hi, I see you've got your kitchen plan in your hand."

"Hello, there are some great colours to choose from."

These truism statements (not questions!) are simple and highly effective. In the customer's mind they will be saying 'yes' or 'that's right' to all these statements and beginning to feel that you understand them.

None of the truisms above are deniable and this helps the customer to accept the salesperson's first comments as truthful and acceptable. Although conversation has begun, there is no obvious attempt at influencing or manipulating the customer into a particular course of action. When you do this, you ease into a conversation, gently avoiding the chance for rejection.

We have here the beginnings of a conversation that has started in a non-confrontational manner and has the potential to continue constructively.

Some prospective customers come into a sales environment with 'resistance' on their minds. For these customers, truisms can be effectively used to agree on a range of issues that they are not **initially** willing to accept from you.

Compare the truism approach with the phrase, *"Can I help you?"* When the answer from a prospective customer is, *"No thanks, I'm just looking,"* we have inadvertently created a barrier to further discussion.

Truisms are effective, simple to use, and a great way to build up natural rapport.

Development Activity

- *Practise truisms in your sales team. You are allowed to enjoy teasing each other!*
- *Create your own truisms appropriate for your sales environment.*

Bridging Questions

Once we have begun the process of rapport building through the use of 'act as if', clean language, and truisms, the challenge for the professional salesperson is to then extend the relationship with the prospective customer. From a truism platform we can then create a natural link into the qualification process (Step 2) by asking a good *bridging question*.

The process of rapport and trust building is underway – now we can begin to find out what is going on in the customer's mind, and get her chatting.

Bridging questions ask the customer to reveal some of her thinking about her prospective purchase. Remember, the prospective customer has come into your outlet for a reason, and the reason is that she is at least *interested* in making a purchase, and maybe even *committed*!

Examples:

"I see you're looking at the bunk beds – do you have children?"

"You've got your kitchen plan in your hand there – what sort of kitchen are you after?"

"There are some great designs to choose from – what type of conservatory are you looking for?"

"It's fun sometimes to try out a new settee – what type of suite are you planning to buy?"

'This model is on special offer at the moment – are you thinking of buying a 600cc bike?"

You can also build a bridge by simply introducing yourself and saying something like:

"Hello there, my name is Nick, what brings you here today?"

"Hi, I'm Nick. What would you like to know about this XXXX?"

Here's a tip – if you have a finance information leaflet in your hand you can also gently plant a seed about an easy payment plan at this stage.

Bridging questions are used at an early stage in the sales process to get people chatting. We are at the stage where a True Professional will enquire in a way that is helpful to a customer and demonstrates interest. We want to encourage the prospect to start talking.

Development activity

- *Practise bridging questions in your sales team.*
- *Create your own bridging questions appropriate for your sales environment.*
- *Review how successful you are at getting the prospective customer to do the talking.*

Trust Building –
What You *Don't* Need

Our unconscious mind always protects us. Its purpose is to protect and it does so around the clock, seven days a week, for the whole of your life. It is a remarkable piece of engineering. Your unconscious mind works tirelessly to keep your breathing and pulse operating when you sleep, as well as staying alert for any signs of danger. We take its protection for granted!

Customers are looking for a trusted adviser. One of the most powerful ways of influencing a potential customer (with integrity) is to build a trust that allows the unconscious mind to relax its obsessive, fanatical grip on protection.

An effective ways of doing this is to highlight *what you don't need*.

A colleague of mine suffered a little knock to her car, which necessitated the purchase of a new front bumper. In the repair shop, she expected the usual sharp intake of breath from the mechanic before he announced the cost of replacing the bumper.

Instead, she was pleasantly surprised when the mechanic told her she could replace the bumper in one of three ways: she could have an original bumper from the car's manufacturer, she could try a scrap yard or she could have a replica bumper from another manufacturer.

All three options had different price tags attached to them and the mechanic told her that she didn't really need to buy an original part as a replica one would look just as good for a lot less cash. Since the idea of trawling through scrap yards didn't appeal to her, she was really impressed by the mechanic's honesty. This is a classic example of building trust with a customer using a 'what you don't need' approach.

'What you don't need' builds trust by advising a customer not to spend more than necessary. It is a wonderful way of reducing any tension or anxiety that the customer may be feeling. Later in the sale process, when its time to think about link-sale items, this trust-building process will help the customer consider add-on purchases as value-adding options, presented by the salesperson with genuine integrity.

Rapport Breaking

Folks, don't be interrupting your customers when they are talking, OK? You've gone to so much trouble to build rapport, and when you interrupt someone in mid-flow you break the spell of rapport and cause damage to your relationship.

Let them finish, no matter how much they ramble on!

10

step 2
understand
needs

Understanding the Customer

We need to understand the needs of our prospective customers through what is sometimes called 'qualification'.

In his excellent book, *'The 7 Habits of Highly Effective People'*, Stephen Covey suggests a habit that fits well in the field of professional selling:

> *"Seek first to understand and then be understood."*

True Professionals do this – it's part of qualifying a prospective customer. They uncover what is going on in the thought processes of the prospective customer before they unleash the stunning features of the product they have in mind to sell. Poor sales operators get poor results because they focus on the product, rather than the customer.

Smart sales professionals adopt a consultative approach. It's not about racing through a sales process and charging towards the close. It's a more measured and structured approach. There needs to be some 'love and understanding' along the way.

In order to understand prospective customers, we need to think about the world they live in, the circumstances of their lives and why they have visited your store or showroom today. Big-ticket retail goods have, by definition, big-ticket price tags, so the motivation for customers to visit your showroom has to be sufficient for them to at least *consider* parting with a large sum of cash.

There must be a reason for their visit.

The prospective customer is seeking a solution to a problem that is troubling her. It might be the style of kitchen she has 'hallucinated' for her new home, a furniture suite, a new mobile phone, the holiday she would like, or a new car she is considering. In each case, a mild inner turmoil is troubling the customer – what should she do? It is the task of the true sales professional to help her to think through her options and find a solution that helps her to resolve her 'troubling' problem.

HALLUCINATION

Be A 'Buying Doctor'

Imagine if a doctor prescribed a course of medication before conducting the investigative diagnosis – there would be an outcry! The same rules apply in the buying process. Professional salespeople conduct their examination of the 'patient' before they start thinking about the right solution for them.

You have developed your bedside manner with the rapport building process – now it's time to examine the customer to find out the nature of her condition.

'Act As If' and be a Buying Doctor.

Emotional Drivers™

EMOTIONAL DRIVER

It is a truism that all human behaviour has a positive intent – that is, people do things for a reason. The reason is not always obvious to the outsider and sometimes is not even consciously recognised by the person exhibiting the behaviour.

Behaviour (including buying behaviour) is driven by an underlying emotional need – an Emotional Driver™ - encouraging us to make a planned movement towards psychological pleasure, or a movement away from existing or anticipated psychological pain.

Although we are not always consciously aware, there is also a physical feeling associated with psychological comfort or discomfort. Scientists have proven time and again that the 'feel-good factor' very quickly translates into physical well-being. By contrast, when we feel down or temporarily depressed, we sometimes experience symptoms of physical illness.

Prospective customers may be eagerly seeking the 'feel-good' associated with a new big-ticket purchase. Alternatively, a potential customer may be feeling physical discomfort when they think about their current 'old' product – maybe a tatty kitchen, a battered car, a dilapidated house, or yet another computer crash?

So, emotion influences human behaviour.

Our emotions and the physical feelings they evoke can be highly influential in our buying decisions. Behaviour is driven by our emotions.

Some businesses I've worked with like to call the Emotional Driver the *Buying Motive.*

A key skill for sales professionals is to uncover the *real* reason why a prospective customer has taken the trouble to visit your store and potentially spend a significant amount of cash. There is *always* a reason. What is it?

Development Activity

- *When you last had a powerful urge to change something at home, why was it?*

● *What possible Emotional Drivers do you think prospective customers may have when they visit your store?*

Emotional Driver™ Example

Some years ago I was working with a group of sales advisers in a well-known home improvement chain. Bill, one of the delegates, was explaining to the group why he spent a big chunk of money on his new bathroom suite. He described his old bathroom:

> **Bill:** "It was dark and dingy. The bathroom suite was really old, that awful avocado colour. There were cracks in nearly all the tiles around the bath and sink, and there was mould everywhere. The carpet was a dark maroon colour and it was stained and frayed at the edges. Every time I put my hand on the bathroom door and opened it, I felt bad. It was sort of depressing. And I thought how awful it was for my children having to get up each morning and use that depressing room. I knew I had to do something about it eventually."

I asked Bill: *"In what way did you feel bad? Where was the feeling?"*

> **Bill:** "In my chest and in my stomach – it felt sort of heavy."

> **NDK:** "How do you feel now, as you describe that experience?"

Bill: "I can feel it now, how I felt then, it's horrible!"

NDK: "What caused you to do something about it – to decide to buy a new bathroom?"

Bill: "One morning when I woke up and went into the bathroom, it was just too much for me. My daughter was outside wanting to use the shower – I could see the shower had black mould in the tile sealant. I couldn't stand it any more. I actually felt guilty that my daughter would have to use the bathroom. I said to myself, 'That's it, I can't have my daughter using a dirty shower, I'm changing this bathroom,' and I made my mind up there and then to go and get it sorted".

NDK: "How much did you spend?"

Bill: "Just under three thousand pounds"

NDK: "And remind us, what was the tipping point for you?"

Bill: "My little girl having to use a dirty shower."

NDK: "Now that **is** a power*ful Emotional Driver!*"

Bill agreed he had been exhibiting '**movement away**' behaviour when he made his decision. A '**movement towards**' Emotional Driver may have had him dreaming of what a lovely new bathroom might look like, or how pleasurable it would be for his daughter. In Bill's case he wasn't hallucinating a new bathroom in terms of what he wanted, it was simply a revulsion reaction, a response to the pain he felt when he thought of his daughter in a grimy shower and the feeling he experienced each time he used the bathroom – a classic case of a 'movement away' Emotional Driver.

Our emotions are a response to stimuli around us. Stimuli cause *feelings* inside us. It is these feelings that motivate us to take action, including buying behaviour.

Development Activity

- *How useful do you think it would be if you could discover your potential customer's Emotional Driver?*
- *What Emotional Drivers have caused you to make a big-ticket purchase?*

Good Questions
(To Uncover the Emotional Driver)

Even sales superstars don't always isolate the core Emotional Driver of a visiting customer, and you may not get all your customers to open up to you, either.

However, by asking good questions you have a much better chance of a customer divulging her inner motivation for (potentially) making a purchase. If you can get to a reasonable level of understanding, you will be in an excellent position to satisfy the customer's need to either move towards pleasure, or to move away from discomfort – whichever is the driving force behind their visit to your showroom.

A good strategy for uncovering a customer's Emotional Driver is to 'start with the end in mind'. Get the customer to think about the whole project ... how will it look, how will it feel, even what it may sound or smell like.

Something as simple as, *"Tell me about the project you have in mind,"* is a great way to get people chatting about *why* they want to buy a new big-ticket product.

> *"I want a bathroom I can relax in after a hard day's work. I love bubble baths and fragrant candles."*

> *"I want a sit-on lawnmower that won't cost the earth. I can't manage the whole garden with the hover mower any more."*

> *"I want the loft conversion done professionally. We desperately need more space and I want to feel that it has been done by a specialist company."*

Asking better questions will allow you to uncover what people want and don't want. Here are some examples:

> *"Can I ask why you are replacing your car?"*

> *"Can you tell me about the things you definitely want in the new bedroom or perhaps the things you want to keep?"*

> *"Can you tell me about the things you definitely don't want in your new kitchen?"*

You can pre-frame these questions with a statement like:

> *"So that I can understand your needs and give you better advice and information, I'd like to ask you a few questions … is that OK?"*

There are five types of questions to consider during the 'uncovering' process:

Open Questions

Open Questions start with a word that encourages 'storytelling' by the customer.

> *"What kind of suite are you looking for?"*
> *"Why are you changing your car? "*
> *"When are you planning to make the change?"*
> *"How are you planning to pay for your holiday?"*
> *"Where will you be riding the bike?"*
> *"Who will be using the computer?"*
> *"What did you like about your old kitchen?"*
> *"What do you not like about your old bathroom?"*

Open questions are just that; they are wide open, leaving plenty of room for customers to answer the question in any way that is relevant for *them*.

When you allow customers room to answer in a way that is relevant for *them*, this provides you with a wonderful opportunity to listen to the words, phrases and messages they convey. Shut up and listen carefully and you'll be surprised what nuggets of gold the customer will divulge to you.

Rudyard Kipling had a simple poem for remembering open questions:

I keep six honest serving-men
(They taught me all I knew);
Their names are What and Why and When
And How and Where and Who.

Probe Questions

Probe Questions explore specific parts of the customer's story in greater detail. Open questions will have created a response with valuable customer information. To find out more, we need to delve a little deeper. By 'probing' with good questioning we can add some flesh to the bones we have already uncovered.

Probing is about being specific. Sales professionals do everything they can to *really* get inside the world of the customer. Probe questions help to discover more about specific aspects of the customer's life.

"You say it will be your partner using the laptop. What will he use it for, primarily?"

"OK, could you tell me some more about what you'd like to include in your new bathroom, please?"

"What a wonderful way to celebrate your silver wedding! What are the essentials you really must have on this trip of a lifetime?"

"Starting with a blank page is a great idea. What is there

about your current kitchen that you'd like to keep in your next one?"

"The models you've been looking at all have multiple shots per second. What sort of photographs do you plan to take with an SLR?"

"The suspension differs slightly between the two models. How would you describe your driving style?"

These probing questions reveal more about the customer and help you to gather valuable 'intelligence' for later retrieval.

Instant Replay Questions

If customers have already behaved in a certain way, they have the knowledge to repeat the behaviour. If you've done something once, chances are you can do it again – you already know how to do it.

Instant Replay Questions uncover the buying behaviours a customer used on a previous occasion (or occasions). We can use this as 'accepted practice', to help the customer repeat the same buying behaviour. As 'accepted practice', the subject will usually find it easy to repeat the same buying behaviour pattern.

Naturally, you will want to establish if the customer's decision-making processes have changed over time. You can combine Instant Replay with a follow-up question to determine whether there has been any shift in decision-making strategy since the original buying process. If there has been a shift – good, we know that we need to adapt our approach. If there has been no shift – double good, we now know with some certainty that this is the most effective selection procedure for our prospect and we can adapt our presentation style accordingly.

> *"How did you decide to buy your last holiday? What is important to you this time?"*

> *"What were the decision-making factors for you when you bought your last car? What is important to you this time?"*

> *"What were the criteria you used when you bought your last house? What is important to you this time?"*

Freedom Questions

Freedom Questions ask about the nature of possibility. They open up fresh thinking about what might be possible. Freedom questions have the magical ability to unlock potential, create new possibility, and sometimes release the hidden or suppressed ambitions of a customer. They are based on two simple questions:

1. *"What would happen if ... ?"*

2. *"What would have to happen ... ?"* (*" ...to make that happen?"*)

For example:

> *"What would happen if you did go on holiday to the Maldives?"*

"I understand you have a monthly outgoing to consider. What would happen if you didn't go for the top of the range model and you were to take the financial pressure off yourself with the more economic model?"

"What would happen if you could afford it?"

"What would happen if you didn't have the extra unit and went for the American fridge-freezer?"

*"What would happen if you **did** order the bathroom that you really want?"*

"What would have to happen for you to decide today?"

"What would have to happen for the entertainment centre to be affordable?"

"What would have to happen for you to be comfortable with that?"

"What would have to happen for the conservatory to be stylish enough?"

Closed Questions

Closed Questions are an essential part of the sales process. They work well because at some point we need to help the customer to come to a decision!

Closed Questions are ideal for beginning the process of bringing the exploratory phase to an end by 'closing down' stages of the sale in anticipation of moving on to the next phase. Specific and targeted questions encourage decision and therefore commitment.

"Would you like it delivered?"

"Is it to take away today?"

"Do you need insurance for this item?"

"So, it's the leather one you'd like?"

"Is it to be the blue one then?"

"OK, have you decided on the size?"

"Good, so that's the seating agreed on, but what about trim? Fabric or leather?"

"Shall we place the order?"

Hallucinations

Customers hallucinate the big-ticket product they are thinking of buying. They create a future world where they have the fabulous product they are dreaming of and experience a *feeling* as a result.

We all hallucinate future events. You have hallucinated many times about what some *where* will be like before you visit, or what some *one* will be like before you meet them for the first time.

In anticipation of a purchase, prospective customers conduct their own dream world construction of what it would be like to own a new big-ticket product (or experience the big-ticket service) in vivid imaginings. They have a mental vision of what the new product will look like, sound like, feel like and even smell like. You've probably done the same yourself when anticipating a major purchase you have been excited about.

Some big-ticket retailers quite rightly refer to 'selling the dream' – a euphemism for 'hallucination'.

To really understand the customer's ambitions it would help if the sales professional could share the same hallucination as that visualised, heard, felt or smelled by the customer – a tough call.

A True Professional will undertake a questioning process to uncover the reasons for the purchase, and maybe even the underlying Emotional Driver that has motivated the customer's visit today.

The difficulty here is that in the process of understanding, the following sequence of events occurs:

Customer hallucinates herself owning the new product,
sometimes in a specific set of circumstances

Customer communicates the product she wants to the sales
professional using her own language to express her desires

Sales professional then formulates his own hallucination of the
customer's hallucination

The sales process proceeds with these inevitably differing
hallucinations in place, with the probability of
'crossed-wires' communication

Being aware of the differences in hallucination is a first step to being an excellent sales communicator. It is important that the hallucinations be brought as close together as possible – so, we need to 'get inside the customer's world'.

You can ask good questions that have the effect of encouraging the customer to help you.

"It's helpful if I can create a picture in my own mind – can you tell me some more about what you would really like?"

"OK, how would you describe that?"

"What would you like to include ... ?"

Inside the Customer's World

Carl Rogers, the influential psychologist, knew a thing or two about rapport building. He said,

It means entering into the private perceptual world of the other and becoming thoroughly at home in it. It involves being sensitive, moment by moment, to the changing felt meanings which flow in this other person, to the fear or rage or tenderness or confusion or whatever that he or she is experiencing. It means temporarily living in the other's life.

(Excerpt from A Way of Being *by Carl Rogers. Copyright I 1980 by Houghton Mifflin Company)*

In sales, the True Professional builds and maintains rapport by temporarily living in the customer's life. True Professionals really understand their customers. They ...

- get inside the customer's world
- find out what is driving the customer to consider buying
- understand movement towards or away
- see things through the customer's eyes
- put themselves in the customer's shoes

IN THE CUSTOMER'S SHOES

- look at things from the customer's standpoint
- use the customer's language
- stand (or sit) like the customer
- think like their customer
- imagine they *are* the customer they see in front of them
- understand what it's like to be motivated by the Emotional Driver that caused the customer to visit today

So, how can you do this?

Fuzzy Language

When it comes to accuracy of meaning, the English language is an imprecise and blunt instrument.

FUZZY LANGUAGE

Most linguists will agree that English is a flexible language, in that it can be adapted to describe ideas through the use of complex sentence construction. However, English, like many language systems, has limited individual words to describe ideas. As a result of the limitations of language, we often find that a word can be interpreted in different ways. In the process of communicating accurately it is important that we have precision.

In sales, it is vital that we gain as accurately as possible a close approximation of the customer's hallucination. The imperfections of the English language make this challenging for the sales professional. Customers, just like everyone else, use what is called 'fuzzy language'; that is, language which can have two or even multiple meanings.

Take a look at the phrases below. These words describe the types of new kitchen customers are interested in buying. Remember, each customer has a vivid hallucination of what she is dreaming of. Each descriptive word is entirely valid in the mind of the customer (and perhaps you the reader) and yet there is a vagueness about the words that allows ambiguity and difference in meaning to exist, and leads to that most dangerous of selling strategies – assuming you know what the customer means.

Is your hallucination the same as that of your prospective customer?

"I want a new kitchen. I want a kitchen that is ... "
- *stylish*
- *modern*
- *contemporary*
- *farmhouse*
- *natural*
- *older style*
- *functional*
- *classical*
- *classy*
- *smart*
- *homely*
- *fresh*
- *trendy*
- *family friendly*

What precisely do these words mean?

A True Professional will recognise these descriptions as being fuzzy and will make a mental note to ask good questions to gain greater precision of understanding and a more accurate reflection of the customer's hallucination.

Using the word 'specifically' is a good starting point.

"When you say 'family friendly', what do you have in mind specifically?"

"Well, no sharp edges for my toddler to bang into, and something to stop him getting into the cupboards."

Or

"What specifically do you want to include in your 'farmhouse' kitchen?"

"I want the split door thing on the outside door, solid wood worktops and a big oak table in the middle of the room. Oh, and some stone floor tiles."

Sales professionals use fuzzy-language-busting questions to gain clarity and a better understanding of the customer's hallucination.

Development Activity

- *What fuzzy language do your customers use?*
- *What 'fuzzy-language-busting' questions could you start using with customers?*

Needs Versus Wants

What a customer needs and what she wants are often very different things.

Let's think about an exciting big-ticket purchase that many people have experienced – buying a car. What you need and what you want can be different.

The table below illustrates some of these differences:

Needs	Wants
• hatchback with four doors and tail gate • five seats minimum • child locks • group 10 insurance, or lower • 35 mpg combined cycle, or higher • minimum 1 year warranty • hi NCAP safety rating • less than £15,000 purchase price • low maintenance costs	• electric windows • central locking • air conditioning • parking sensors • smart CD/music centre • leather seats • alloy wheels • less than four years old • hands-free phone kit fitted

Needs and *wants* are fundamentally different, although they are both driven by emotional leverage:

● **Needs** – are the essential 'security requirements' that are the minimum a product must offer in order to be considered. Needs usually include pragmatic, practical features described in relation to constraint, movement away from fear, or feelings of safety and security.

- **Wants** – are exciting and pleasure enhancing. These are the attributes of a product that add glamour or added appeal. Wants are often aspiration-based, offer movement towards pleasure and 'feel-good factor', and are often far from being a pragmatically essential product or service feature. Wants are powerful drivers in the process of selling despite their apparently non-essential nature. Wants stretch customers' willingness to pay – people will pay surprisingly large sums of cash for something they *really want.*

Incidentally, some people will buy on wants alone! A friend of mine recently bought a fabulous Harley Davidson motorcycle – a truly beautiful machine. Did she *need* it? No. Did she *want* it? Oh, yes! The Want was such a powerful Emotional Driver (look cool, sound cool, feel good) that she paid thousands of pounds for the Want.

Both Needs and Wants are driven by an urge for 'feeling'. It is just that the motivator feelings differ in form. By understanding the nature of Needs and Wants in the mind of your customer, you can use this information productively during the sales process.

Needs tend to be emotional-logical, whereas Wants are emotional-excitable. You can use both sets of motivators in the sales process. One of the simplest ways of uncovering the difference in the mind of the customer is to ask her:

*"What are the things you really **need** in your new conservatory, and what would you really **like to have**, if you could?"*

*"What is **essential** for you to include in this world cruise, and what would you **add in** if you could?"*

*"What do you think you absolutely **must have** in the kitchen design, and what would be an **added bonus**?"*

*"What features will you **need** for the entertainment centre, and what would really **make it special** for you?"*

My guidance to you is to sell to the Need first – if there is one – and then get on to the exciting Wants!

Development Activity

- *What (do you assume!) are typical Wants and Needs of your customers?*
- *What good questions could you ask for uncovering customers' Wants and Needs?*
- *How can you engage people's Wants?*

Different Strokes for Different Folks

The development activity above hints at a common error of sales-people – making assumptions about customers' Needs and Wants.

It is (another) truism that each customer is unique and has her own values, beliefs and personal motivators, including the all-important Emotional Driver for making a big-ticket purchase.

Take a look at the character 'differences' shown on the next page and ask yourself how many of them might influence a person's buying behaviour:

Different Customers, Different Values, Different Beliefs

- what they/we find funny or sad
- who makes what decisions and in what circumstances
- how and when they/we use means of transportation
- what is modest or risqué
- when, where and how they/we sit and stand
- what's considered common courtesy
- what's polite and impolite
- whether people are in control of their lives of if fate determines this
- how closely we stand to each other
- the holidays they/we celebrate and how they/we celebrate them
- what makes 'common sense'
- what are worthwhile goals in life
- what is beautiful or ugly
- the roles of men and women and how each should behave
- whether conversation should be formal or informal
- how they/we perceive what is friendly and unfriendly
- how open or guarded they/we are with information
- what behaviour is ethical and unethical

Credit where it's due – this is an adaptation of *Global Competence: 50 Exercises for Succeeding in International Business*, a training manual from HRD Press edited by George Simons, Selma Myers and Jonamay Lambert.

The answer, of course is 'most of them'.

True Professionals are attuned to personal variances in belief and values. They understand that people have their own 'maps of the territory' and take care to navigate carefully as they begin to pick up hints and messages during conversation. Professionals listen and watch for clues. Failing to consider these differences can be damaging to the sales process.

There is danger in a busy sales environment of transferring our own characteristics, or the characteristics of a previous customer, or generalisations about 'customers', on to a new visiting prospect. In doing so, we run the risk of making assumptions.

Professional salespeople understand that each prospect presents a completely different challenge and opportunity from the previous one. They adapt their behaviour and communication style accordingly; starting afresh with each new person they meet. Smart sales professionals 'wipe the slate clean' or 'start with a blank canvas' with each new prospective customer.

Development Activity

● *Think about two or more recent customers. How did they differ?*

What Would You Pay?

How much would you pay for a new pair of shoes? Really? I wouldn't pay that much. Or maybe I'd pay much more. You don't know.

PRICE ACCEPTANCE

Each customer is different and has his own map of what is a reasonable price for a product or service. Finding out the *Price Acceptance Map* of your customer is a valuable starting point for any big-ticket sales activity. Price acceptance may relate to overall price, or possibly to monthly spend, term of a finance arrangement, APR sensitivity, or possibly to one specific element within the big-ticket sale.

Finding out the starting point for price acceptance gives you a marker to refer to. It doesn't mean the customer will stay there – it's just a reference point. Good questions can uncover the Price Acceptance Map as well as steer customers towards different ways of paying that they may not have considered.

"What are you expecting to spend on your new holiday?"

"What are you thinking of investing in this home improvement?"

"What sort of monthly spend are you thinking of?"

"How much will you be willing to invest in this?"

"How much are you planning to put aside each month?

I think £10,000 is a lot of money to spend on a kitchen or conservatory, but when I think of it as an investment in my property, adding long-term value, I'm much more open to a payment plan that costs a couple of hundred pounds a month for a few years.

It's all about identifying the Price Acceptance Map as an

initial marker and then helping a customer shift the map to reflect the perceived benefits of your fabulous product.

Remember, everyone is different. One customer may think £10,000 for a big-ticket product is expensive. Another customer may think it is super value.

Development Activity

● *Find a friend and ask him for his thoughts on price acceptance for the following big-ticket products. What would he pay? Compare his thinking with your own price acceptance map.*

What is your price acceptance map for ...

Big-ticket Item	Price range?	Acceptable monthly payment?
a new car?		
a new bathroom?		
a new laptop?		
a new bicycle?		
a new piece of exclusive jewellery?		
a new music system, TV, or home entertainment centre?		
a new kitchen?		
new windows all round?		
a holiday?		
a new house?		

The B Word

I hear many sales people in big-ticket environments using the word 'budget', as in, *"So, what is your budget?"*

We need to think about the words we use. The word 'budget' has a number of meanings for people. Think about how the word 'budget' could be interpreted by a customer:

- budget = cheap
- budget = low cost
- budget = poor quality
- budget = association with 'hard times'
- budget = government speech with taxation news
- budget = amount of cash available, or 'monthly outgoings'

None of these experiences of the word 'budget' are positive, inspiring or exciting. They will not evoke feel-good in the customer.

People buy a big-ticket product or service because of what they want to feel. Remember, their purchase is an investment in feeling as a direct result of their Emotional Driver. People buy big-ticket products to achieve feel-good, either from movement away from pain, or as a planned movement towards pleasure.

They are putting aside an investment in feel-good.

"What sort of investment are you thinking of making in your new conservatory?"

"What are you thinking of putting aside each month as your investment in your new (product name)?"

"What are you thinking of spending on this investment?"

"What are you expecting to invest in order to own a new sports car, like this?"

"Are you planning to buy with cash or would you prefer to make a gradual investment with a sensible finance arrangement?"

An 'investment' has long-term benefits, with an associated feel-good.

Development Activity

● *What language patterns can you use with your customers that include the word 'investment'?*

Up To ...?

Most prospective customers will offer what professional negotiators call the 'initial settlement point' as the financial ceiling for their investment in your big-ticket product or service. Almost all customers will go beyond this initial offer if encouraged to do so.

The *'Up to ... ?'* language pattern is a nice way of uncovering the upper end of a customer's planned investment. Once the sales person has asked for an outline figure that the customer is expecting to invest, and a figure has been mentioned, the sales person simply asks the question, *"Up to ...?"* with a quizzical expression and then waits for a response.

The 'Up to ... ?' language pattern is not guaranteed to reveal the absolute maximum spend, but it does give you a better chance of stretching the initial figure offered to you by the customer. The pattern works whether the figure referred to is a lump sum, or a monthly investment.

It works like this:

Sales person: "What sort of investment are you thinking of making in your new conservatory?"

Customer: "About ten thousand pounds."

Salesperson: "Up to ... ?"

Customer: "Up to about twelve, I suppose."

Or

Sales person: "What are you thinking of putting aside each month as your investment in your new (product name)?"

Customer: "Four hundred, four fifty, something like that."

Salesperson: "Up to ... ?"

Customer: "Well ... I definitely don't want to spend more than five hundred a month."

"Up to ... ?" is a great way to up-sell with elegance.

Development Activity

- *Practise "Up to … ?" next time you ask a prospective customer about his planned investment.*

Constraints

There are usually some parameters to work to in making a big-ticket investment, and not just those associated with financial matters. Customers will have some constraints within which their new product of service will need to fit. The True Professional will incorporate these constraints into the sales process thinking regarding 'customer needs'.

Asking good questions will help uncover constraints that may exist.

Constraints might include:

- timing to fit personal circumstances, e.g., house move, building works, holidays, new job, timing of cash availability
- size or shape of room/garage/work area
- need to accommodate children
- safety non-negotiables
- compatibility with other products
- insurance restrictions
- external space
- health/disability issues
- lifestyle factors
- combining business and social use
- other users of the product/service
- restrictions imposed by partner, e.g., colour, brand loyalty

Constraints are usually restrictive. A True Professional will respect constraints and present a product solution that fits nicely within the parameters described by the customer. This will prove helpful later in the sales process when it comes to summarising your understanding and presenting a proposed product solution that fits perfectly with the customer's needs and wants.

IMPORTANT: Do not allow financial parameters to dominate your thinking about constraints (we'll come back to finance later).

Development Activity

- *What are the typical constraints that customers have when considering a big-ticket purchase from your portfolio of products (other than price)?*

Must Haves

Must Haves are those essential features of a product that a customer finds irresistible. Chances are, you have experienced the 'must have' mentality when you've been considering a new big-ticket product yourself.

- The new car that *must have* leather seats.
- The new kitchen that *must have* soft-closing drawers.
- The new bathroom that *must have* an installation service available.
- The home entertainment system that *must have* speakers in each room.
- The conservatory that *must have* blinds.

- The new house that *must have* a garage.
- The new dining table that *must have* an extendable/removable mid section.
- The holiday that *must have* water sports activities for the children.

Must Haves are an important feature of most people's big-ticket requirements. They don't always make a great deal of sense, and they aren't always associated with a clear benefit. However, the prospective customer has a Must Have in mind, and your job as a True Professional is to provide the Must Have and satisfy the customer's requirement. You can identify the Must Have simply by asking for it,

> *"Is there something that you simply must have in this new XXXX?"*

Development Activity

- *What might be the Must Haves of a customer in your sales environment? Remember, everyone is different!*

Desirables

Along with the *Must Haves* are the *Desirables*. This is the 'Want' rather than the 'Need'.

Desirables are those features of a product that add sexiness. They are the things that 'would be nice to have'. If you can get some of the desirables into the product mix for the customer you are offering a tantalising and teasing proposition. Remember, people get excited about Wants much more than they are Needs, and being able to have a Desirable as well as the Must Haves might just swing if for you.

Listen out for *Desirable* language:

- It would be great if the new car *could have* sat nav.
- It would be great if the new kitchen *could have* a Rangemaster oven.
- It would be great if the new bathroom *could have* a wet room.
- It would be great if the home entertainment system *could have* a home cinema.
- It would be great if the conservatory *could have* a nice tiled floor.
- It would be great if the new house *could have* solar-powered heating.
- It would be great if the new dining table *could be* mahogany.
- It would be great if the holiday *could have* a hire car included.

You can identify the Desirable simply by asking for it,

> *"Is there something special that you would really like to have in this new XXXX, if you could?"*

Development Activity

- *What might be the Desirables of a customer in your sales environment? Remember, everyone is different!*

Is There Anything Else?

This is a really important question to ask. You've done your level best to find out everything that's significant for this customer in considering the purchase of your fabulous big-ticket product. No matter how hard you work, there's always the possibility that you've missed something or the customer forgot to mentions something.

"Is there anything else … we need to think about … we need to take into consideration … that's important to you … that you'd really like … that you want to avoid … " is a great way to mop up anything that has slipped through the net in the qualification process.

Development Activity
- *Practise using "Is there anything else?" at the end of your Understanding Needs investigation process – it will pay dividends later.*

The Decision Maker

A really important part of the qualification process is to determine if you are talking to the decision maker! You might not be.

Sometimes you will be selling to someone who is on a 'scouting mission' on behalf of themselves and their partner. Some prospects will have the authority to make the decision themselves, but it makes sense to check out if they will be doing their own 'internal' selling job when they get home. It's best to establish this early on so that everyone knows where they stand.

These are good questions to ask about the Decision Maker:

"Who else do we need to consider regarding this purchase?"

"Will you make the decision to buy, or do you have to consult anyone else?"

"Is there anyone else who needs to agree with this, or can you decide yourself?"

If your prospective customer is going home to 'sell' the purchase, you have an opportunity to ask about the things that are important to the absent partner, and to help him prepare for his own domestic sales process!

"What will your partner be looking for, do you think?"

"What is important to your partner?"

"What is your partner likely to ask you about the (product)?"

You may have to encourage the prospect to revisit with his partner – and that's no problem at all. We just need to be clear on what's what.

11

step 3
demonstrate

Order Takers

Some customers are great! One of my friends bought a car a few years ago. She walked into a dealership and said,

> *"I'd like that car there, the one in black. I have the cash available today and I want to take delivery as soon as possible."*

The sales executive couldn't believe his ears!

> *"Would you like a test drive, madam?"*

> *"No, I would like to **buy** it please!"*

Wow! Wouldn't it be fantastic if we could have all our customers lined up ready to buy like that! We wouldn't be True Professionals then, though, would we? We'd be *Order Takers*.

Some salespeople operate as Order Takers as their standard procedure, and that works fine when a product is in such high demand that supply can't keep up. It's not often this happens though, and demand exceeding supply rarely lasts long. That's why smart salespeople understand the value of professional demonstration.

Features and Benefits

Most salespeople are familiar with the concept of features and benefits. Even the most basic sales training highlights the importance of distinguishing between what a product or service does, and what that means for the customer in terms of benefit.

Despite this, the application of this knowledge seems to fall short of most sales organisations' expectations. It seems that many salespeople struggle with making the connection between a feature and the benefit of that feature.

Incidentally, the classic features and benefits model sometimes includes a third component, Advantages, as in Features, Advantages, and Benefits. My guidance to sales managers and trainers of salespeople is to avoid Advantages. It is too much for most salespeople. Many can't cope with making the simple connection between a feature and a benefit – let's not make it even more difficult with a third concept.

Stick to Features and Benefits.

Brochure Giving

Oh, I love the *Brochure Givers!* These are the salespeople who have so little skill, such low levels of confidence, or are so lazy, that they give out a collection of photographs to do the demonstration phase for them.

BROCHURE GIVER

You'd be surprised at some of the world's most prestigious brands that employ salespeople who just give out brochures. I don't expect that's what the retail businesses *really* want them to do. Giving out a product leaflet or brochure as your primary demonstration strategy will provide poor results.

Professional selling is a structured process and the product brochure is a useful sales aid if you don't have any real product. Brochures can be useful if a prospective customer is on a first visit and needs a reminder of the quality of your product when he is at home later, considering his choices. Brochures can be great reference reminders, and attaching your business card will give a direct contact number for the prospect, too.

It will not do the demonstration job for you though, so please don't use it as your prime demonstration strategy. There is a better way.

Feature Dumping

Because so many salespeople find it personally challenging to connect between features and benefits, they resort to *Feature Dumping*. Feature Dumping is the (all too common) process of dumping a list of product features on a poor unsuspecting customer.

Feature Dumpers pride themselves on their product knowledge and then download as much information about product features as they can recall, often in no logical order. The intention is to impress the customer with the extensive features of the product and then wait for a hallelujah moment when the customer will say,

> *"Oh, my word, how wonderful, please let me buy one immediately!"*

What really happens is that the Feature Dumping results in an internal *"So what?"* response from the customer. Some folk just fire off an elephant gun full of grapeshot (the *Grapeshotters!*) hoping that if they tell the customer absolutely everything about the product that surely something relevant must hit the target!

Feature Dumpers and Grapeshotters are inefficient, ineffective, unprofessional and naïve.

GRAPE-SHOTTER

Feature Dumping Dave

Read this genuine transcript of a salesperson ('Dave' – not his real name) in full Feature Dumping mode in the process of 'selling' a kitchen. The conversation was recorded as part of a video mystery shopping campaign commissioned by a national retail chain. Dave is a full-on Grapeshotter.

As you read the transcript, consider the understanding that Dave gains about the customer's needs, wants, must haves, desirables, constraints and the all important Emotional Driver as he feature dumps all over the prospect. Take a deep breath, because you'll need it ...

"Hello, can I help?'

Prospective customer: "Er, please, yeah, I'm thinking about some new bedroom units. I think I need some advice."

Dave: "OK, great!"

Prospective customer: "I'm just looking at some of the ones in pine or oak. I'm looking for an idea on what's available, and prices, of course."

Dave: "Right, I'll show you. What we do is we run a system where we can let you choose the bedroom in different parts and such like. You buy your units and you choose the finish you want ... are you with me? We can do that with this bedroom and this one and this one, right? This range has doors with these handles and you can't change them like you can with some of the other ranges. They're pre-drilled for the doors but not for the hinges, though. I'll show you the others. Of course, if your existing bedroom cabinets are all right you can just put new doors on and you can just take them away and fit them, or if they've had it we can do the full job and we can fit them too. We can do whatever you want. And then there's the bed itself, of course … "

Prospective customer: (interrupting) "So … "

Dave: "You can mix and match what you want. These units come at this price here and you have to decide what sort of finish you want because that will dictate the price, like, and you can have us fit it, but probably it will take about seven to eight weeks for us to do it at the moment. All these ranges, here, come as a set bedroom with what you can see here, so you can't separate it into bits, it's just as it is, like. Then there's the solid woods and the laminates and these are much more expensive than the laminates. Those cheaper ones come as they are with what you can see, for the price, like. Some people are happy with that, like, and some prefer a bedroom that they make up themselves, as it were, but then there's the cost to consider … "

Prospective customer: (interrupting) "So, are the units all the same with each … "

Dave: (interrupting) "All the cabinets are just the same, it's just what finish you choose, that's the difference, because you can choose what you want, as long as you go for a dearer one. This one is laminate and it's a cheaper price than the solids, but then some people want that. And it depends if we fit it for you or you do it on your own, because that will impact on the price, I mean you might want to go for an expensive one and fit it yourself or you might want a cheaper one and we can fit it for you or you might have someone to do it for you. Take this brochure, it's all in there."

Prospective customer: "Oh, all right then, thanks ..."

And so, sadly, the sale was lost.

Development Activity
* *Do you Feature Dump?*
* *If yes, stop doing it immediately.*

Fit With Emotional Driver

Feature Dumping doesn't work. Poorly trained and coached salespeople Feature Dump. They go to great lengths to explain the features of their product, irrespective of the relevance of those features to the prospective customer.

The True Professional understands that the demonstration phase of the sales process must be tied back to the Emotional Driver of the customer, the movement away from discomfort, or the movement towards pleasure that the prospect is seeking and which has motivated him to visit your showroom.

It makes sense then to demonstrate the features and benefits that relate directly to the movement they desire. There's plenty of time to add in a few extra sexy features and benefits that the customer may like to learn about (save the really good ones for later in the demonstration phase), but let's get the primary driver dealt with first – the Emotional Driver.

Start your demonstration with what's called a 'pre-supposition'. A pre-supposition pre-supposes that something is true. It presents an idea in an assumptive way that most customers will accept as an accurate statement:

"One of the nice things about this model is ... "
"What's great about this is ... "
"One of the things our customers say they like is ... "

Remember though, that a truly influential demonstration will relate back to the Emotional Driver you uncovered, or part uncovered, earlier in the sales process. We need to tie together the demonstration of features and benefits to the movement away or movement towards.

Take a look at these examples:

Demonstrating fit with the
Customer's Emotional Driver

Emotional Driver	Features and Benefits
I do a lot of miles and I'm fed up with the fuel bills, I want something more economical.	What's great about this particular model is that it will achieve 65 mpg (F). That will lower your fuel bills substantially (B), and as well as that, your servicing will be free for the first two years (F). That's more economical (B), and it's a new car too.
I want a really nice acoustic guitar for my son that he will feel proud of, at a price that I can afford.	One of the appeals of this guitar is that it is a GGG, one of the best acoustic brands you can buy, at a sensible price (F). Your son will be proud to own and play this one (B) and it won't cost the earth (B).
I want to be able to relax on a Sunday morning with the papers.	One of the nice things about this conservatory is its spaciousness – it has room for a chair and settee (F). It is the perfect place to relax on a Sunday morning with the papers (B).
Safety is important to us – we'll be using the car for the school run.	What's really impressive about this model are the safety features. The car has an automatic braking system (F) that prevents the wheels locking from up if you have to brake hard (still F). It means you stay in control even if you have to jam on the anchors (B). There are seven air bags too (F) so you can have peace of mind (big B!).

Emotional Driver	Features and Benefits
The door hinges in my kitchen keep dropping, and the shelves are falling to bits – it's driving me nuts.	What's reassuring about these door hinges is that they are so strong (F), they will keep your doors in the correct position (B), and the shelves are designed to hold up to XX kg (F) so you don't need to be driven nuts any more! (B)
I don't have time to keep painting my windows each year. I want some new ones that will last a long time.	What's nice about these UPVC windows is that they will last for many, many years without any maintenance (F). You don't have time to paint windows (B).
I'm looking for an exclusive piece of jewellery that no one else will have.	One of the lovely things about these pieces of jewellery is that they are handmade and individual (F). No-one else will have one of these designs (B).
I've always wanted a XXXX and now I think I can afford one.	It helps of course, that we are specialists in XXXX and have plenty of models for you to choose from (F). It's great that you can now afford what you've always wanted (B).
I've got a large family and I want to take my children on a foreign holiday in the sun that includes a flight. They've never been on a plane before and I really want them to experience the excitement. I think I can get about £3,000 together.	One of the terrific things we can offer is such a wide choice. We have lots of foreign holidays that include a flight (F). Let's see what we have for you and your children that will include a sunny destination and the excitement of a flight, at a price you can afford (B).

Development Activity

- *Think about the profile of your customers.*
- *What might be a typical Emotional Driver a customer would come to you with?*
- *How do the features and benefits of your products fit with this Emotional Driver?*
- *Consult with a colleague, what do they think?*

Sense Selling

When a customer considers a potential big-ticket purchase, she undertakes a mental assessment using as many of her senses as she can usefully engage.

SENSE SELLING

Scientists call this VAKOG assessment, where

    V = visual (visual attractiveness)

    A = auditory (how attractive it sounds)

    K = kinaesthetic (how it feels to touch, and how it makes the customer feel 'inside')

O = olfactory (how it smells – think 'new car smell')

G = gustatory (how it tastes, where it's appropriate to taste it!)

In the process of big-ticket selling it really does help if you can engage as many of a customer's senses as possible. Of course, it's not always practical to engage *every* sense. The challenge for you, as a selling professional, is to do the best you can with your product to allow the customer to use as many senses as possible during her 'assessment'.

Let customers see the product, hear it in use (including how silent it might be), touch and handle it, adjust the controls if available, and smell that 'new product smell'. If there is an opportunity to taste the product, good for you!

Car retailers know the power of a customer sitting in the car, holding the steering wheel and 'playing' with the switchgear.

Phone retailers know the importance of letting the customer handle the mobile phone and test the features.

Furniture retailers encourage customers to sit in the settee or run their hand over a smooth wooden surface.

Musical instrument retailers know that musicians (or *wannabe* musicians!) like to play the instrument.

Motorcycle retailers know that bikers like to sit on the machine.

Top of the range entertainment centre retailers know that customers like to use the remote to experience sound quality.

Food retailers know that 'taste tests' are a great way to hook a new customer onto their product.

Development Activity
- *What are the VAKOG elements of your product?*
- *How can you use them during demonstration?*

Test Driving

When you test drive a car you get to try-before-you-buy. Customers like to try out big-ticket products before they commit to a sizeable investment. It makes sense to do so.

You know from 'sense selling' that customers respond most positively when they can use a combination of senses to decide whether to buy. Test driving takes this to another level. By giving a prospective customer the opportunity to use elements of the product, you are bringing her closer to the reality of ownership, and what that will *feel* like. Remember, people buy things to avoid a feeling, or to access a feeling. It's the Emotional Driver within all of us.

Let's think of a few examples of 'test driving' a product. Notice how the examples given include a good helping of 'touch'.

Test Driving Your Products

Cars, vans, trucks	Sit in the vehicle, adjust the seat, handle the controls, and then go for a test drive!
Motorcycles, watercraft, bicycles, other 'sit-ons'	Sit on/in the vehicle, handle the controls and then (if possible) test drive
Conservatories	Open windows, pull up/down the blinds, sit in a comfortable chair

Kitchens	Open and close doors and drawers, pull out carousel units, handle 'knobs', adjust lighting
Bathrooms	Open shower doors, adjust showerheads and taps, handle accessories, lie in the bath!
Furniture	Sit on chairs and sofas, extend tables, activate electrically adjustable recliners
White goods	Open the doors of fridges, freezers, washing machines, dishwashers etc, handle accessories
Premium electronic products, including computer equipment	Handle demonstration equipment, use service features
Entertainment centres, TVs, and audio products	Handle remote control, change channels, adjust volume, listen to favourite music, use specialist features, sit comfortably and enjoy
Mobile and landline phones	Handle phone handset, use features, practise using keypad
'Upmarket' jewellery	Try on the jewellery, handle the product, and look in the mirror!

Development Activity

- *How could a customer 'test drive' the performance of your product range?*

Good – Better – Best

Good – Better - Best is used extensively in sales to present a range of products of differing quality and different price to a prospective customer. Each product has a set of features and benefits reflecting its quality standard.

- **'Good'** is usually a baseline product offering minimum features and little else. An analogy is the 'basics' food products offered by supermarkets, e.g., *Value/No Frills Baked Beans.*
- **'Better'** product lines have some perceived added value benefit with an increase in price. Continuing with the super-market analogy, most supermarkets offer own-label food products presented as a 'quality' product.
- **'Best'** is just that: the top-of-the-range product line from a market-leading and prestigious brand with added features and benefits and a top-line price.

Presenting Good-Better-Best offers the customer choice and a logical reasoning between each standard of product. As the customer moves along the value chain from Good through Better, to Best, so the price increases, and in most cases so does the profit margin. In big-ticket, the price increases between each are more significant and so are the margins.

Big-ticket retailers know that margin is vital and will encourage customers to move towards a higher value product wherever possible. Most BTR businesses have Good-Better-Best product lines.

What is important in selling Good-Better-Best is to be clear on the features and benefits of each product, so the customer can understand the differences and make an informed choice. Always start with 'Good' and work your way up the value chain, offering greater value as you present each product to the customer.

The process of comparison is important, as it allows your prospective customer the opportunity to compare one possible solution to another and to select a best fit by a process of elimination. Some big-ticket retailers will call this technique 'up-selling', as the sales professional takes a basic purchase by the customer and suggests *even better* product options further up the chain.

Some sales processes suggest starting with 'Best' – what is sometimes called the *Premier Product* or *Showcase Model*. They argue that 'gravity' takes over and that although the customer will back off from the top specification, he will settle on a product option somewhere below the Premier Product demonstrated.

I disagree. I think that is 'down-selling' and is based on selling by price, not value. I think you should work up the Good-Better-Best chain, adding value as you go. The message to the prospective customer is:

> *"Yes, it does cost a little more, but that's because you get so much more!"*

Offering Good-Better-Best provides plenty of choice within your retail operation. It encourages a customer to consider which one of a range of products he finds the best fit for his needs and wants. The implicit message is:

> *There is no need for you to consider going anywhere else for your new big-ticket product, because we have such a great*

range of products, of varying quality and price. You can make your decision with us.

The Good-Better-Best technique is a version of what is known as an *'Alternative Sale'*, because the customer is presented with a choice of possible purchases, all of which have their virtues. Of course, the fourth option – 'none of these' – is not presented.

Development Activity
- *What are your Good-Better-Best product lines?*
- *What are the differences in features and benefits of each product line?*

Amplification

When a customer makes a positive or complimentary comment about your product or service, you have a wonderful opportunity to employ *Amplification* as a sales influencing technique.

Amplification is a technique used to deepen rapport with the customer while strengthening the perceived fit of your product to her Emotional Driver.

It works by simply repeating back the complimentary comment made by the customer and then 'amplifying' the comment by adding an adjective that strengthens the original comment. For example:

Customer: "That's smooth, isn't it!"

Sales professional: "Yes it is, it's <u>really</u> smooth!"

Or

> **Customer:** "Oh, that's good value."
> **Sales professional:** "That's right, it is <u>really</u> good value!"

Or

> **Customer:** "That's clever!"
> **Sales professional:** "You're right, it is <u>very</u> clever!"

Amplification is effective in encouraging a sale because it does the following:

- It confirms to the customer that the product has excellent attributes.
- It utilises *Clean Language* (the customer's precise phrases – and if possible, tone of voice).
- It confirms to the customer that you were listening.
- It confirms to the customer that you are genuinely interested in what she thinks.
- It confirms to the customer that she was right in her evaluation.
- It confirms that, in fact, she was *even more right* than she first thought.
- It strengthens customer ego and makes her *feel good* about the buying process – and you.
- It makes it easy to move effortlessly to a *Trial Close* (more on *Trial Closing* later) and then to a full *Close*.

Development Activity

- *Practise using amplification with your customers and experience just how influential this technique is. You'll find it effective. In fact you'll find it really effective.*

'Big Up' Your Finance

Most big-ticket retailers have a finance facility to aid the process of buying.

This is a wonderful opportunity for the True Professional because it offers more choice to the prospective customer who may have a limiting belief (a 'Straw Prison') for herself around the 'B' word – *budget.*

Most customers have some idea of overall cost for the big-ticket product or project they are interested in. For many this will be a generic 'round' number that they have imagined as being roughly relevant to their intended purchase. The challenge is that this number is often built on little more than guesstimate and is rarely accurate.

The *Straw Prison* they create will feel real to the customer, as though she cannot break out of it, even though it is simply a number she has chosen in her mind.

It helps to know what this number is. If you have been diligent in your 'understanding of needs' Step 2 phase you will know what this rough figure is already.

When it comes to the actual price of the big-ticket product or project, knowing the customer's Straw Prison figure will result in one of two things:

1. **The product/project will be significantly *less* than the customer expected.**
   Unprofessional salespeople sell down to a customer's planned spend. The True Professional, once she knows the customer's planned spend, will offer add-ons that work back up to the number the customer has in mind.

In effect, *"You've got what you wanted for the price you wanted to pay, and you get all these extras too!"*

Or

2. **The product/project price will be significantly _more_ than the customer expected.**

In this case, we have work to do in either changing the product/project specification, or more preferably, changing the way the customer feels about price and payment.

Different methods of payment help customers to break free from their Straw prisons, especially when they consider the long-term gains that most big-ticket products and projects offer.

At the demonstration phase, it's probably best not to get too embroiled in finance options. Simply to flag up the opportunity to be 'a little creative' with how the customer can *comfortably afford* the product they aspire to own. You *plant the seed*. The purpose at demonstration time is simply to introduce flexibility into the thinking processes of the customer. Nothing more. Be a *Seed Planter*.

This approach provides a little more leeway when it comes to demonstrating a product range and means you can introduce a wider scope of choice to meet the Must Haves and Desirables of your prospect.

Make sure you 'Big Up Your Finance' by being a Seed Planter – it really will help your customers get what they want.

Development Activity
● *What are the features and benefits of your finance offers?*

Floppies

We all say things from time to time that undermine our credibility. Things are going well and then we go and say something stupid. We've all done it. In sales situations a *Floppy* is a language pattern or utterance that undermines our sales proposition.

FLOPPIES

Poorly trained salespeople occasionally offer uninvited and damaging Floppies relating to what the product or service **does not**, **will not** or **cannot provide** for the customer. Why salespeople need to inform the prospective customer of a negative benefit is unknown; it may be an urge to 'be honest' with the prospect or perhaps it is an unfortunate side effect of the *Feature, Feature, Feature* mind set. They get so carried away that they even want to tell the prospect what the product *can't* do for them!

We've all come across this as customers ourselves. White goods salespeople are talented at explaining when products can't be delivered by, and some retailers are experts in the art of advising customers what sizes they don't have in stock. It seems almost self-sabotaging and yet there is consistent and compelling evidence that salespeople are drawn towards this self-defeating strategy.

We come across Floppies in everyday language when people use tentative, floppy words that dilute the impact of a message. We hear words like 'hopefully', 'probably', or even worse, 'possibly'. These words, and others, such as *might, perhaps, try, expect so, I'll do my best, fairly,* or *reasonably* undermine the verb or sentence that follows.

> *"I hope to have that in stock later this week … "*
> *"I'll try to get the package to you tomorrow … "*
> *"It should be OK … "*

These are all weak, insipid, floppy words that inspire little confidence in the listener. My guidance to you is to choose words that suggest a definite, positive outcome. Your unconscious mind will react in a more definite fashion, too, once you choose a direct approach:

> *"I will have that in stock later this week."*
> *"I will get the package to you tomorrow."*
> *"It will be fine."*

We sometimes fall foul of Floppies, inadvertently, when we communicate with customers. Many salespeople use apologetic language that automatically conveys tentative and uncertain messages. The outlook is not promising when a salesperson starts a sentence with phrases such as,

"Unfortunately … "
"Sadly … "
"I'm afraid … "
"I'm sorry to say … "
"I'm sorry, but … "

When we use Floppy language we are unconsciously setting up the customer for disappointment. They know from the sentence construction and the tone that what is coming next is bad news. My guidance to you is: avoid Floppies and stick to the positives!

Yes and the Best Way …

In big-ticket selling, it is unusual for prospective customers to make a purchase over the telephone without first viewing, feeling, hearing or smelling (the new car smell?) the product. The challenge is to get the prospect from the other end of a telephone to the showroom or store.

There is a simple language construction that aids this. Negotiators, politicians and assertiveness coaches know the power of the repeat button. They simply replay the same language pattern time and again until the message sinks in to the recipient. You may have heard politicians when they are questioned on television or radio. They have a pre-prepared sound bite that they replay over and over again, irrespective of the question being asked.

The same principle applies in big-ticket sales, when we really need the prospect to come and visit us to view the product. The pattern is simple to understand and straightforward to use. It is an ideal sales strategy for responding to direct, closed questions asked over the telephone.

It follows a question from the prospective customer such as, *"Does it have a warranty?"* or *"Is it economical?"* or other such closed question.

The pattern starts simply:

> *"**Yes, and** ... '* and then continues, *'**the best way** for you to ... see/feel/experience/hear that ... is to **come in to the showroom** ... "*

You can use the same pattern when asked an inquisitive question such as:

> *"How economical is it?"*

> *"It's very economical ... **and the best way** to check that out is to **come in to the showroom** and we can look at the figures together. When would be a good time for you to pop into the showroom?"*

Development Activity

- *Would you like to know more about this language pattern? Does it actually work? Yes it does, and the best way for you to really embed it is to come to one of our training seminars and we will help you learn how to use it ...*

12

step 4
summarise and
recommend

Fit With Emotional Driver

At Recommendation time, you will make a firm proposal about the specific product that you feel best fits with the customer's needs and wants, constraints, desirables and must-haves. But before we start recommending, let's think about where we've got to in the sales process.

Remember, everything comes back to the Emotional Driver, the *movement away* or *movement towards* motivator of your prospective customer.

It's just as important to tie back your recommendation to the Emotional Driver as it was during the Demonstration stage, if not more so. We need to remind the prospective customer of the reason why he has visited your showroom today. This is a critical phase in the selling process and it is vital that the prime motivator for the customer's visit is satisfied by your proposition, so make it obvious!

> *"You said it frustrates you when you see your large garden overgrown and you don't have time to mow it regularly. This XXX model sit-on mower will do the job in a jiffy. It will feel different when you see it nicely mown."*

> *"You said owning a XXXX product would make you feel like you've achieved a lifetime dream. Let's see how I can help you to own a XXXX and you can have that feeling. Would you like that?"*

Development Activity

● *Practise your language patterns, developing a recommendation format that ties back your product to the customer's Emotional Driver.*

Names

By now rapport should be being built up with your customer – it's time to deepen it by sharing names!

> *"I'm sorry, I don't know your names ... I'm Nick ... (offer handshake). Hi."*

If you're lucky your customer may offer his or her name. If he or she offers a name, such as as 'Mr Raichura' or 'Mrs Raichura', use 'Mr Raichura' or 'Mrs Raichura'. If he or she offers a first name, such as 'Nuj' or 'Shaheen', use 'Nuj' or 'Shaheen'. Of course, if he or she doesn't offer you a name, that's OK – he or she may just be a little reserved, or maybe you don't have the depth of rapport you thought you had!

Let's be positive and assume you've been successful in building up sufficient rapport for you to use names. Now you can use their names during the summary phase!

Summarise

Its time to gather up all the information you've discovered about your prospective customer, his Emotional Driver and the movement he seeks, his needs and wants, his constraints, desirables and must-haves, and the product or service options you've explored together that fit with these requirements. It's time to summarise what you've both learnt.

There's a very simple strategy to achieve this. You simply say, *"OK, let's summarise ... "* and then proceed to do so.

A summary helps to reduce the likelihood of objections or 'customer concerns' later on. It gains incremental agreement on the things that are important to your prospective customer.

Yes Sets

An elegant approach to summarising is to use a *Yes Set*. The Yes Set serves two purposes:

1. It engages the customer in the summarising and agreement process.

2. It gains a series of 'yes' responses to your questions that build up a momentum and predisposes the prospective customer towards saying 'yes' to your questions, including the all-important *Close* question.

Here is a typical Yes Set,

"OK, lets summarise ... let me see if I've got this right ... you said you have just moved in to your new home and that you're not keen on your current bathroom. That's right?"

"Yes, right."

"OK, you said you've always wanted a wet room rather than a basic shower unit and you want a retro freestanding bath with legs. Correct?"

"Correct."

"We've had a look at your room dimensions and we've found a layout design that allows us to fit these in to the current bathroom. And you're happy with the layout design we've come up with?"

"Yes."

"Good. OK, you said you must have wall-mounted taps and you want us to install the new suite for you. Is that right?"

"That's right, yes."

"Excellent, so we've looked at the XXXX range and the YYYY range, and both of these suites do what you want. You said that of the two, you preferred the YYYY suite. Have I got that right?"

"Yes, I like the look of that one."

"You wanted (note past tense) *to stay within £2,000 – and you may consider taking advantage of our finance arrangement for convenience's sake. Have I got that right?"*

"I might do, yes."

Your customer is starting to feel that you have a really good grasp of her needs and that she is being well cared for by someone who knows what they are doing – a True Professional.

We now have a track record of agreement with the customer that has also strengthened our rapport. This is good progress. Now we need to strengthen our position further with an indirect suggestion that fits with the customer's Emotional Driver.

Development Activity

- *Take a summary that is typical in your sales environment and break it down into smaller parts, securing a 'Yes' response (or similar such as 'Correct', 'That's right', etc.) at each stage.*
- *Practise, practise, practise!*

Indirect Suggestions

Once the *Yes Set* is in place you can start to reinforce your proposal and create a bit of leverage with an influential indirect suggestion. The timing for an indirect suggestion is ideal after a good solid Yes Set.

An indirect suggestion presents an idea to a customer in a way that encourages a buying decision. Used with integrity, a well-placed suggestion will help the prospective customer to recognise the benefits of your product or service and smooth the way towards a sale.

Detailed below are a dozen different styles of indirect suggestion you can choose to use with prospective customers – so there's plenty of choice for you! Remember to be as natural as you can in your language and adapt the examples given here to suit your normal style of communication.

The True Professional will, of course, select an indirect suggestion that is a best fit with the Emotional Driver of the prospective customer.

Few sales professionals use all of these suggestions, so read them through and choose one or two you'd like to use and then practise, practise, practise, until you are competent in their use. You can then go on to practise a few more. Before you know it, you'll be a master of indirect suggestion!

1. The More the More

The More The More suggestion model is based on *'the more that something ... then the more that something else'*. The pattern also works well with *'the more ... the less'*, *'the less ... the more'* or even, *'the less ... the less'*. The more you practise this pattern, the more you'll find how influential it can be!

Sales Suggestions:

- *"And **the more** you use it, **the more** comfortable you will find it ..."*
- *"And **the more** you think about it, **the more** you will realise how much pressure this will take off you ..."*
- *"Of course, **the more** accessories you buy, **the more** personalised you can make it ..."*
- *"**The more** you order now, **the less** you will need to re-purchase later ..."*

2. Covering All Possibilities

When we want to focus a customer's mind towards a particular solution, it is helpful if we can suggest a limited set of choices. *Covering All Possibilities* is a suggestion technique used to help prospective customers choose from a restricted range of responses that still provides choice. The available responses, however, are all focused towards one of the products in your range.

Sales Suggestions:

- *"I don't know which of these models you prefer ... whether you should decide on the teak or mahogany or ash woods ... because only you can decide which is the best natural wood for you ... natural wood is something you've always wanted ... whichever you choose will be the right choice ... which do you think you'd prefer?"*
- *"You may wish to choose the three night stay or the four night package for you and your partner ... you could book now while our room rates are on special offer ... and before they go up ... or you may wish to consider the weekend special ... which one do you think would be best for you?"*

- *"You can choose from any one of these speaker systems ... they all offer fantastic sound quality ... which you say you've always wanted ...it really comes down to style and price ... which ones appeal to you most?"*

3. Comparing Opposites

Comparing Opposites is a great way to highlight just how wonderful your big-ticket product or service is. By contrasting the new against the old, or compared to an inferior product, there will be an automatic 'gap' that really shows the added value your proposition will offer.

Sales Suggestions:

- *"Yes, it's a lovely new kitchen with strong hinges as you asked ... how does it compare with your old one?"*
- *"How does this YYYY brand entertainment centre differ to your current sound system?"*
- *"It's such a large spacious house ... ideal for your growing family ... of course you could always choose the small, claustrophobic one we saw earlier!"*
- *"You said you are impressed by its smoothness ... and smoothness is important to you ... how does the smoothness compare to your old car?"*

4. Not Knowing, Not Doing

Not Knowing, Not Doing is a well-proven language pattern that makes it easy for a customer to buy. Not Knowing, Not Doing helps the prospective customer relax because there is so little for her to do – the stressful activities normally associated with buying a big-ticket item are taken away from her.

Most customers are busy people. They will find the invitation to not do, or not know, too inviting to resist and so accept your kind generosity to 'make it happen' for them.

Sales Suggestions:

- *"There's no need to worry about installation ... just tell us when is convenient and we'll do all that for you ..."*
- *"And you don't even know yet, how much simpler life will be ..."*
- *"And without knowing, you will have reduced your heating bills ..."*
- *"And you don't have to do anything at all ... we will arrange it all for you ..."*
- *"You don't have to get a screwdriver anywhere near there; it's all assembled for you ..."*
- *"You don't have to worry about delivery ... we will arrange that for you ... you don't even have to pay now ... we can delay the payment ... until you are ready ..."*

5. Forgetting Confusion

Forgetting Confusion helps prospective customers to 'remember to forget' the sales presentation of your competitors. Forgetting Confusion is a useful tool to create competitive advantage, by suggesting that your product or service is a simple and an obvious solution compared to the complex presentation given by a competitor.

Sales Suggestions:

- *"Some other companies try to baffle people with detailed facts and figures ... there are so many details they have to tell you ... it can be confusing and easy to forget ... **now** ... fortunately, our product is very simple to understand ..."*
- *"Sometimes it's best to start again from scratch ... forget what you've been told so far ... what is it you want to achieve ...?"*

By the way, it's best not to identify or refer to competitors individually when adopting this strategy. Customers often think that criticism of a competitor is disrespectful and mean. Do you want your prospective customers to think that about you?

6. Trigger Suggestion

Trigger Suggestions are powerful tools to help prospective customers remember your product or company, when they encounter some physical experience in the near future.

TRIGGER SUGGESTION

Suggestions can be given directly, by instructing the potential customer that when they encounter a certain experience, they will immediately think of you, your product, or your company.

Sales Suggestions:

- *"When you get back home and look into your garden ... you'll remember our meeting and how wonderful this conservatory would be ..."*
- *"When you hear your partner's voice on the phone ... you'll remember our discussion about this cruise holiday, won't you?"*
- *"When you get in your car ... from now on ... I think you will remember this test drive ..."*

7 and 8. Revivification

Revivification is a technique used to help people 're-live' a particular experience in an intense fashion – so intense that they really feel that the experience is actually taking place again. There are two revivification models to consider:

7. Positive Revivification

In *Positive Revivification*, a customer is asked to remember a time when she was experiencing *feel-good* associated with a product or service similar to the one she is considering purchasing from you. We want to help the potential customer recall a positive state of mind and to feel good about what we want to talk to him about … our fantastic product!

The customer is asked to recall the experience, and to revive or 're-live' the sounds, sights and feelings from the events that took place. We want the customer to be back in that positive mind-set. This suggestion works really well when a natural conversation is taking place and the customer is discussing past experiences in a relaxed and friendly way.

Sales Suggestions:

- *"Do you remember when you got your first motorbike?"*
- *"What was it like?"*
- *"What did it look like?"*
- *"What was it like to ride?"*
- *"How did you feel when you first got on it?"*
- *"A wonderful feeling, by the sound of it! I think we can help you to feel like that again, with this brand new motorcycle …"*
- *"Do **you** remember a particularly lovely holiday from your childhood?"*
- *"What was so lovely about it?"*

- *"How did that make you feel?"*
- *"A wonderful feeling, by the sound of it! I think we can help your children to feel like that with a skiing holiday ..."*

8. Negative Revivification

In *Negative Revivification,* the technique utilises past circumstances to illustrate how your product will help avoid an unpleasant future experience. It is the combination of revived past pleasure and a fear of potential negative future experience that creates the leverage.

It is useful to recognise here that anxiety is a powerful motivator. You can help your customer avoid anxiety through the benefits of your product or service. Negative Revivification is closely associated to the 'moving away' principle described earlier.

Sales Suggestions:

- *"You said you want a phone that doesn't lose its charge as quickly as your old one ... you've had enough of it driving you mad, as you said ... **it was really annoying,** I know ... well this phone is amazing, it will keeps its charge for (x time) so there's no need for you to feel that frustration again."*
- *"You said you missed the property you really wanted when it was on the market ... because you didn't want to stretch your finances too far ... and now it is worth so much more ... **you missed the opportunity that time ... and you were frustrated** ... now you have the chance to put that right ... this property may be a stretch ... but think how much you would regret missing this one!"*

9. Future Orientation

Future Orientation is a process that allows customers to think forward to a time when an aspiring set of circumstances may occur. It asks the customer to imagine, hallucinate and experience life in the future.

This is a successful methodology for creating what I call a 'compelling future' or 'wonderful obsession'. A compelling future draws the customer towards an exciting set of possibilities: new car, new home, etc. and allows her to enjoy the feel-good associated with the future state.

We tend to get what we focus on. By creating a compelling future customers will move towards it.

Sales Suggestions:

- *"I wonder how will this look ... when you drive it ... into the golf club car park?"*
- *"Now ... if you can see yourself sitting in this conservatory ... on a Sunday morning ..."*
- *"Now ... when you and your family will move in to your new home ... it will be a special day ... what will you be feeling ... I wonder how different it will be ..."*

10. Dissociation

In its simplest form, dissociation is the separation of mind from the surrounding environment. This is something we do every day when we focus on a task, read a newspaper or book, or concentrate on something specific. We dissociate when we daydream or drift off into 'another world'.

For the purposes of the sales professional, creating dissociation is important. We want the prospect to be dissociated from the wider environment because we would like him to give 100 percent of his attention to our proposal or presentation.

Professional salespeople know that distractions can often 'break the spell' when we are at the critical phase of a presentation or pitch. Despite our best efforts, a ringing phone, outside noises, vehicles in the street or voices in another room can distract from the sales process. The challenge for the accomplished sales professional is to incorporate distraction into the sales process. We want the distractions to aid the prospect to concentrate fully on our presentation.

The key here is to utilise everything that happens to create dissociation in the prospect. Distractions are an opportunity to *double* the intensity of interest!

It can be fun too. Try these indirect suggestions with a smile on your face!

Sales Suggestions:

- *"The more that car alarm sounds, the more you can appreciate just what a difference this kitchen will have for you and your family ..."*
- *"Even the phones seem keen to know about this new range of ours!"*
- *"Let's leave those voices to drift away and look at the real benefits to you of this style of conservatory ..."*
- *"Ah ... children's voices ... they'll love it when they see their new loft bedroom ... just like this one in the brochure ... how good will that be?"*

11. Time Distortion

Time distortion is used to help customers speed up or slow down their perception of time. We have all experienced our reality of a holiday 'flying by too quickly' or 'waiting forever' for a train or bus – or a spouse!

In a sales environment, it is often important to make presentations seem brief for the customer. In this situation, a skilled sales professional using time distortion techniques will 'set up' the prospect for a time distortion that shortens his experience of the presentation.

Sales Suggestions:

- *"This is a really exciting presentation that will fly by ... so I need your full attention for the next few minutes ... I will explain the benefits pretty quickly ... we will need to progress at a rate of knots ... shall we get going quickly ...?"*
- *"We have a few minutes ... and that's OK ... we only need a few minutes ... we can take our own time ... together ... we can use time wisely ... let's focus on the benefits for you of this product ... now ..."*

12. Repetition

Repetition is one of the most direct and effective suggestion techniques. In politics, spin doctors have known of the power of simple repetition for many years. Listen on radio, or watch television, and you will quickly pick up the language patterns of politicians who have been trained to repeat key messages again and again and again. In British politics, Tony Blair will be remembered for his pledge to voters, *"Education, education, education."* The same principles can be employed in sales.

Sales Suggestions:

- *"It's about value ... great value ... this is our best value model ..."*
- *"Fast? This is really fast ... I rode it and I couldn't believe how fast it is compared to last year's model."*
- *"The key here is safety ... safety ... safety ..."*
- *"You want something hard wearing ... this one has a hard-wearing worktop ... it's a really hard-wearing surface ..."*

A Word About Integrity

The key principle in making suggestions in sales is personal integrity. The question must be, *"Does my product or service genuinely offer value to this customer?"* If the answer is *"No"* then why are you trying to influence the prospect in the first place?

The True Professional works with integrity.

If you don't believe in your product and don't believe that your potential customer would benefit from it, then you are operating outside of integrity and you will have to live with your own ethical model of the world. If you truly believe in your big-ticket product and you genuinely believe that the prospect would gain real benefit, then you are helping him to buy something that will add value to his life. *That* is selling with integrity.

Development Activity

● *Practise the use of indirect suggestions with prospective customers until you become elegant with their application. You'll be surprised how effective they are. Imagine how successful you will be as you use indirect suggestions. In fact the more you use them, the more you'll discover your sales improve. And you don't even know yet, how much simpler selling will be ...*

Based on What You've Told Me

You've made some good indirect suggestions to the customer using one or more of the language patterns described above; now it's time to be direct and make a firm recommendation that you think is a best fit for the personal circumstances of your prospect based on what you've discovered.

The recommendation phase is a crucial element in the sales process. By recommending, we are making a direct suggestion to the prospective customer, based on the information provided **by** the customer.

This is why information gathering is so important. We repeat back what we were told, ideally using Clean Language and Amplification to maintain rapport, add in an indirect suggestion or two, and then make an informed 'professional' recommendation. The recommendation is based on the must-haves and constraints of the customer, and with the additional information gained (like, dislike) during the demonstration phase.

A nice language patterns to use is *"Based on what you've told me ..."* and proceed to make the recommendation you think best fits the customer's requirements.

Development Activity

- *Think about the language patterns you would use with prospective customers, given the products and services you have to offer. How would you incorporate the recommendation phrase "Based on what you've told me ..."?*

Price Gaps

Remember, a prospective customer probably already has a rough figure in mind as the 'total price' or 'monthly outgoing' she is willing to commit to.

By following the sales process so far you will have a good idea of what she wants, why she wants it, when she wants it, and what *specifically* she wants. It may be that the product solution you have jointly identified is more expensive than the total investment, or monthly outgoing the customer had in mind.

You'll see the customer's reaction (remember non-verbal communication?) before you hear what she says so you'll know how she feels about the extra cost – if there is any, of course.

The true 'cost' associated with a price higher than the customer expected is actually much less than first feared. In fact, the 'cost' to the customer is just the difference between her anticipated cost and the actual cost of the big-ticket product once it has been scoped up and priced. Why? Because in the customer's mind she had *already* committed to an anticipated price and 'bought' the product at her expected level of investment.

Let's take a look at an illustration:

- product: new bathroom
- customer expected investment: £3000
- actual price of chosen specification: £4800
- cost above expected investment: £1800

Now, in the example above the investment is likely to be enjoyed by the customer for a number of years, maybe three years, five years or possibly even longer.

The significance of this is that the customer is making an investment in her home and that has a long-term benefit – the customer will have years of pleasure from the purchase. This means that we can help the customer recognise that her 'extra' spend per year is actually very little, and certainly worth the investment over a period of time.

- cost above expected investment: £1800
- 'life' of product: five years
- investment above expected spend: £360 per year to get the product *she really wants*

Finance Opportunities

Now is a good time to go back to the finance opportunity. Customers will have a range of payment options in mind, typically:

- cash
- credit card
- finance loan
- lease plan/contract hire (where relevant)

The True Professional will have mentioned finance in the demonstration stage, almost as an aside, and presented it as a *convenience*, a way of 'spreading the cost'. It's a nice question to ask a prospective customer,

"How would you like to spread your investment?"

The way in which we present the finance offer is important. Your prospective customer may have some reservations about using a finance arrangement.

The challenge with a finance plan is the association some people have with the word itself: 'finance' evokes certain feelings in some people. Fears of being persuaded to take on debt that they can ill afford, past experiences, scare stories of mountainous interest rates, memories of being told of the dangers of borrowing money, all contribute to consumer scepticism of finance offers.

'Convenience' is a word that suggests 'taking away *in*convenience'. By presenting your finance plan as a convenience that helps with domestic cash flow you are offering a benefit. It also means the customer can think beyond the restrictions of the 'rough figure' she originally had in mind and look towards the product that she *really* wants.

The influencing effect of group norming can also help the prospective customer feel comfortable about finance. If 'most customers' are using the convenient finance plan it can create a feeling of normality in the mind of the customer if you share this news with her. Of course, you'll want to be honest about this: maybe it's *some customers*, rather than *most*. You decide.

It's really important that you follow the strict guidelines for the manner in which finance is introduced to prospective customers. Most state legislation is in place to protect the consumer and sales professionals should follow it with integrity.

Development Activity
- *You'll want to know the features and benefits of your finance plans. What are they?*
- *Why would a prospective customer want to use your finance plan?*
- *In what way is it convenient, specifically?*

Trial Closing Using Customer Language

By now it's time to test how we are getting on.

A 'trial close', or 'test close', checks out how near a prospective customer is to deciding to buy. By gently testing the attractiveness of part of the sales process, or a specific aspect of the product, you can get a feel for how well the sales process is going.

Good trial close questions might include:

- *"Is that the sort of thing you are looking for?*
- *"Is that the sort of thing you are thinking of?*
- *"Is that the sort of thing you had in mind?*
- *"Does that look about right?"*
- *"Does that feel about right?"*
- *"Does that sound about right?"*

Incidentally, if you've listened carefully you might have heard the prospect using certain language patterns as a verbal habit. Listen out for phrases like

- *"I like the look of ..."*
- *"It sounds ..."*
- *"It feels ..."*

These phrases when used habitually by a prospective customer can be used when communicating back to them to deepen rapport. If the customer consistently talks about 'the look' of things, then ask, *"Is that the kind of thing you are **looking** for?"*

The same rules apply for customers who habitually refer to how '*it sounds* ... ' or how '*it feels* ...'

This is called the *representational system* of the customer (*seeing* language, *hearing* language, or *feeling* language) and you can deepen rapport and trust during the trial close by using the same *seeing, hearing* or *feeling* language they use. It suggests that you *really* understand the customer. It's powerful stuff.

If you get a 'No' response to your trial close question you have some more work to do and you'll need to go back to an earlier part of the sales process and re-check the customer's Emotional Driver, the movement motivators, needs and wants, constraints, desirables, and must-haves. Maybe you need to demonstrate a different product that is a better fit? Have you missed something? Did you misinterpret something? Do you need to ask better questions?

If you get a 'Yes' response to your trial close question, it's decision time for you! Do you go for the 'close' and ask for the order now, or do you add on some additional link-sale items and get a bigger order? How brave are you?

Development Activity

● *Think about stages in your sales process where you could use a trial close. What sort of trial close phrases could you use?*

Link Selling

Link selling is sometimes known as 'add-on' selling. Link selling adds value to your customer as well as increasing your order value. Most big-ticket retail organisations are keen to maximise their average order value (AOV) or average transaction value (ATV) through up-selling (see *Good-Better-Best*) or link selling.

How does link selling add value to your customer?

Think about pick-and-go retail goods stores. Almost everyone has made a retail purchase (think decorating!) and then got home to find they have forgotten a key additional item: wallpaper, paste, paint ... oh, drat, I forgot the paint brushes. The same principle works in big-ticket markets.

You can enhance the experience and the feel-good for a customer by adding on some fabulous accessories. The customer is already excited about his new big-ticket product and now is a great time to help him feel even better by putting the icing on the cake with your link-sale goodies!

It's simple too. The customer is already in a buying mood, so link selling is often an easy soft sell that improves the buying experience for the customer while sometimes significantly increasing the order value.

Just be sure you keep to some key principles:

- Maintain rapport.
- Refer to the main item as if the customer has already placed the order, *"Your new kitchen"*, *"Your new motorcycle"*, or *"Your new bathroom suite"*, etc. This creates an implication of purchase and a suggestion of understandable pride in the product.
- Use what's called a *Statement-Question* language pattern as your opening phrase. A Statement-Question is a two part pattern that begins with a fairly safe truism, such as:
"You'll want to make the most of your new XXXX"
Or
"I expect you will want to look after your new YYYY"

And then follow the statement up with the link-sale question, such as *"How about ..."* as your introduction to the fabulous link-sale goodies. This is a logical thought process that your customer will recognise as a sensible idea.

- Explain the features and benefits of the add-on.
- Ask for the link-sale order, continuing with the Statement-Question approach, *"It makes sense to include ZZZZ. Shall we add that in?"*
- At worst they'll say no; at best the order value will be increased without placing the main order at risk.

And it's OK to keep going with your link selling – some customers will keep buying and buying until they feel they have absolutely *everything* to make the most of their fabulous new big-ticket product. The customer will tell you when you've reached the end point.

Remember, link selling improves the buying experience for the customer. It would be unprofessional of you *not* to help with link-sale suggestions.

Development Activity

- *Think about your main product lines. What are the possible link-sale/add-on sale opportunities that would add value for your customer and increase your order value?*

Link Selling Potentials

Main Product Line	Link-Sale Opportunity

Framing and Reframing

'Framing' is the way we put a perspective on a particular situation, issue, characteristic or behaviour. 'Reframing' is the creation of a new perspective on a particular situation, issue, characteristic or behaviour.

FRAMING

You can take virtually any situation and place either a negative frame or a positive frame around it. It really is your choice!

Epictetus, the ancient philosopher, had a few thoughts on framing and reframing. He knew that it is how you think about things that really matters:

> *"What disturbs men's minds is not events, but their judgement on events."*
> Epictetus, The Enchiridion, c135 AD

If you change the frame on something, you can also change the meaning and if you can change the meaning, then responses and behaviour will also change. The ability to frame positively gives greater freedom and choice.

Positive framing makes the most of a set of circumstances. It's rare that a big-ticket retailer has absolutely every part of the proposition just how they would like it. Sometimes there are a few issues about delivery, or maybe availability at certain times – there's always something to improve in every business.

The challenge for the True Professional is to present the circumstances you work with in a positive manner, with a positive 'frame'.

Here are some examples of negative and positive frames around the same set of circumstances:

Negative Frame	Positive Reframe
"I'm sorry to say that it will be at least eight weeks before we could attempt to get that to you." "I'm sorry, we can't do that for you." "That particular model will push you over your budget."	"The good news is that we can get that to you within eight weeks, so you have plenty of time to make your mind up about paintwork choices and curtains." "What I can do for you is ..." "And what's great is that our finance package allows you to spread the cost so easily manageable."

Development Activity

- *Create a set of positive frames around some of the service issues that bug you.*
- *Photocopy the box below and start practising. You'll be surprised how quickly you get into the swing of reframing!*

Negative Frame	Positive Reframe

13

step 5
close

Closing on a First Date?

Just before you rush off and pounce on all those visiting customers, it's worth thinking about what stage the customer has reached in her buying journey. Research conducted by a number of large retailers suggests that customers rarely commit to a purchase on their first visit to a big-ticket showroom. It seems that consumers are canny enough to realise that the first offer is not necessarily the best deal and that further choices are almost always available.

One robust piece of research revealed that most furniture customers make a buying decision on their third or fourth visit. Customers said they were annoyed by retail sales staff who attempted to 'close them down' when they were visiting only their first or second store. Customers want to look around the supplier base and feel they have a good understanding of what the market has to offer. 'Salesy' efforts by retailers to 'close' were met with resistance and disapproval.

However, once customers have had the chance to review their options, they are definitely ready for decision-making!

An obvious strategy to adopt is to find out where the customer is on the buying journey. Some smart big-ticket retailers now include a filtering question in their sales process. *"Are we the first store you've visited?"* and *"Where have you looked so far?"* are both great questions for understanding where the customer is in the buying cycle and how she should be treated within your own sales process. Some retailers employ a 'greeter' with specific responsibility for uncovering this valuable information.

If this is a first visit, tread carefully – you may meet resistance to a buying decision. If it's a second or third visit, get ready to use your fabulous closing skills!

Of course, every rule is there to be broken and some customers will want to 'buy on a first date'. You already have an excellent technique for testing this – the trial close! You can test the mind-set of the customer with gentle trial closes and then make a judgement as to whether to proceed with your full armoury of closing techniques.

If it is a 'no-close' visit, there is still a lot to be done. We don't let customers go that easily!

ABC

Always Be Closing!

This is a cheesy old sales cliché, but it works. ABC helps to gain clarity and focus if you can work with the customer to gain 'mini-agreements' at each stage of the sales process.

"So, you'd like the Devonshire style if we can get it with the right handles?"

"Yes, I like that style."

"OK, Devonshire it is then."

Always Be Closing gets you nearer to the close well before you enter the close phase. The dialogue above could easily take place much earlier in the sales process, do you agree?

Yes?

Good.

Sales pros know that by gaining a 'yes' at regular intervals you will build up a Yes Set and also save yourself a lot of hard work in backtracking over old ground when it comes to the closing phase of the sales process.

Are we agreed that Always Be Closing is a smart thing to do? Yes?

Good. Let's move on.

Development Activity

● *Practise ABC with your colleagues as a fun activity and then practise with your customers – you'll be surprised how their agreement to your mini-closes leads towards the close itself. Brilliant!*

Ask for the Business

You would be staggered at the percentage of salespeople working for world-class brand names who find it difficult to ask for the order. It's shocking. They can put in all the hard work at each stage of the sales process but they just can't bring themselves to ask for the business.

Poorly trained and coached salespeople become anxious about asking for the order because they fear rejection in the form of a *"No"*. Fear of a *"No"* is understandable if you haven't followed an effective sales process – and quite probable too!

At some point, you will need to ask for the order. In fact, many customers are expecting, even hoping, that you will ask the question. The poor customer is willing the sales guy to ask the question so that they can be 'sold to' – it's the way some people's minds work. Often customers feel embarrassed about 'buying' – they prefer to be asked.

Customers give off buying signals and make comments all the time that invite your 'close'. At the right time in the sales process (that's now) you can spot a genuine buying signal:

BUYING SIGNALS

- nodding as they look at you or the product
- being quiet as they run their hand over the product
- making comments such as:
  "Could you deliver it by next week?"
  "Is it in stock?"
  "How long will it take to sort the finance?"
  "Is the warranty renewable?"

"What's the next step?"

"I don't want any mess. Can you install it when we're away?"

These are all cracking buying signals made at just the right time after you've done your job as a professional by following the sales process through to this moment.

Now it's time to ask for the order!

You have a right to ask for the order – after all, you've acted professionally; you've been friendly; you've asked the right questions; you've understood what is going on in the customer's world; you've checked that you understand; you've demonstrated products and services that you think fit the customer's emotional and practical needs, including any constraints that may exist; you've checked that they fit; you've summarised all of the above and sought agreement at every stage in the form of a Yes Set; and you've made a recommendation that you genuinely believe will help the customer move towards the pleasure that he seeks, or away from the pain he wants to avoid.

Phew! You've <u>definitely</u> earned the right to ask for the order. You are a True Professional!

Here are some potential questions you could ask. Notice how they are mostly closed questions that will lead to a *"Yes"* or *"No"* answer. If you've done your job well and followed the sales process you're far more likely to get a *"Yes"*.

Most of these questions are assumptive questions, where you assume the customer is about to buy. Some are alternative questions, where two or more options are presented as choice for the customer. Again, the assumption is there that the customer will choose at least one of the options.

- *"Shall we place the order for you?"*
- *"Would you like me to arrange delivery for you?"*
- *"Would you like to take it now?"*
- *"Shall we go with that?"*
- *"Shall I take this to the check out for you?"*
- *"Shall we get the paperwork done/out of the way?"*
- *"Can I take it to your car for you?"*
- *"Shall we arrange the installation?"*
- *"Would you like me to book that in for you?"*
- *"Shall we get the delivery in the diary for you?"*
- *"Would you like to order the red finish or the blue?"*
- *"Would you like delivery before Christmas or after Christmas?"*
- *"Would you like to pay by cash or by card, or would you prefer to use our finance plan?"*

If your rapport is really good, rather than ask a question, you can go for a direct suggestion, and even have some gentle fun with a cheeky proposal. Make sure you smile as you say these:

- *"I think you'd better buy it, don't you?"*
- *"I'm going to have to hurry you …!"*
- *"Go on, you've worked all these years, you deserve it."*
- *"I think it's time to treat yourself, don't you?"*
- *"I might have to think about this for you – er, OK, I've thought about it – I think you should buy it!"*

Or the really cheeky direct suggestions,:

- *"Well, I think, **by now** (buy now) we should be ready to place the order!"*
- ***"Right now** (write now) I think we're ready to do the paperwork!"*

Development Activity
● *Which close questions work best for you?*

Deadly Delays

Sadly, not every customer will commit on the day. We know this from research. There are plenty of absolutely valid reasons why people 'want to think about it'.

These *Deadly Delays* might include:

● They want to consult with their partners.
● They want to think about other financing opportunities.
● They want to check out your competitors!
● They don't have the measurements they need.
● The house or room isn't ready for the new purchase.
● They are waiting for a promotional deal.
● Their personal decision-making strategies involve careful consideration away from the sales environment – they genuinely want to 'think about it'.

All of these are absolutely valid reasons for *not* purchasing right now. If you attempt to overcome these Deadly Delays by encouraging the customer to buy on the spot, you risk being perceived as an arm-twisting salesperson and all the good work you've done in rapport building will be lost.

Deadly Delays are inevitable from time to time and no amount of haranguing or 'influencing' will change the prospective customer's mind. Even if you do 'close', it's likely the customer will feel manipulated and suffer from subsequent *buyer's remorse*

– that awful feeling when you realise after the event that it wasn't a very wise purchase, or that you have been coerced by a manipulative salesperson.

The True Professional recognises a Deadly Delay as simply that – just a delay. The True Professional realises that he has an opportunity to maintain rapport and keep the sales process alive, even *after* the prospective customer has left the store, showroom or dealership.

All you have to do is follow up and get the customer back in the sales environment as soon as you reasonably can – having resolved her Deadly Delay.

Follow Ups

Not every customer buys on a first visit. We know that now. Deadly Delays are sometimes unavoidable and in many cases thoroughly understandable. Some customers will go some way down the sales process and still back off from the purchase as they consider their options. That's fine; we can't *demand* that a prospect buys there and then.

What we can do is follow up on the prospective customer's visit by calling him a few days later to check on how he's got on with his Deadly Delay.

The key here is to set up the expectation of a brief call, at a time and date convenient to the customer. This means 'pre-framing' the customer to expect a call from you in a few days' time, or whatever period is appropriate, to *" … see how you've got on."*

Of course, this means you'll need some information, especially a phone number, maybe an address or e-mail address and definitely the prospective customer's name! It helps the communication process if you give your name too.

You can't call the prospective customer, or e-mail her, if you don't secure her contact details while she is still in-store talking with you. Get the data and retain it. It's very simple:

> *"Can I just take your name and phone number? I'll give you a call in a day or two to see how you've got on with your measurements, and let you know of any special offers that have come in. When would be a good time to call?"*

When you make your call (in a few days' time) you'll need to get your rapport back up to speed quickly. It helps if you have a few notes from your initial discussion to refer to, and if you've got some background information, then even better. It's nice to catch up on family circumstances or social news.

> *"Hi Mr Godfrey, it's Nick from ZZZ about the (big-ticket product). We agreed that I'd call you today to find out how you got on after your chat with your partner. How was the weekend away? Did you have a good time?"*

Remember, professional selling is a structured process. You only ever sell from one step in the sales process to the next one. Think about the purpose of your follow-up call. What do you want to achieve? It is most unlikely that you will sell your big-ticket product over the telephone. There is only one purpose for your call, and that is to get the customer back into the store so you can start the sales process all over again.

"OK, excellent. The best way is if the three of us could meet up at the showroom and I can take you through the new range that's just come in, and I can explain some of the great offers we are doing at the moment. When would be a good time for you both?"

By the way, most big-ticket retailers have regular changes to their promotions – chances are there will be some 'good news' to pass on to your prospective customer when you call him, as promised, at the time and day you agreed.

Development Activity

- *Practise your follow-up procedure. Make sure you get the information you need so you can get your rapport back up to speed as soon as possible, and get him back to see you!*
- *Make it a habit to collect and retain prospective customers' contact details.*

Convincers – The Right Choice!

Let's be positive! You've followed your sales process professionally and your prospective customer has agreed to become a fully-fledged customer by placing an order either on the day or as a result of your excellent follow-up technique. Well done! What next?

The *Convincer* is a very useful sales tool for inspiring confidence in the customer.

When a customer has just purchased a big-ticket product, adrenalin is almost certainly running through her veins! Your customer has just made a major investment and a natural reaction is for her to check back and review her actions. She is scanning her behaviour and rethinking the implications of what she has just done. She replays the videotape in her mind.

Naturally, we hope that the check-back and scanning process results in an internal confirmation that she has made the right choice and can be content with what she has done. That's not always the case, though.

Occasionally a customer will experience 'buyer's remorse' and wish she hadn't made such a major commitment. In many countries, consumer laws require that a customer can cancel a purchase within a certain period of time – especially where a financial plan has been agreed. Returns and cancellations are not good for your business.

BUYER'S
REMORSE

As a True Professional, you will want your customer to feel good about her purchase. Some customers are actively seeking confirmation that their actions were sensible. They are looking around for help and relief from their mild anxiety – they want a Convincer. You have a job to do.

It is important to reassure your customer that she has made a wise decision – we need to create 'closure' for her before she leaves the showroom. Explain that you'll call later that day, or in a few days' time, to confirm that all is going well with delivery or, if it is a pick-and-go sale, to find out how she is getting on with her fabulous new big-ticket purchase. This gives your customer a feeling of security – that you are genuinely helping and that you *care*.

By confirming to the customer that she has been wise in her buying decision, you are helping her to proceed through the internal checking process as quickly and painlessly as possible.

Direct Suggestions are useful at this point. A Direct Suggestion is a Convincer made to someone in a firm and assertive manner. In a time of mild confusion or uncertainty, such as immediately after making a big-ticket retail purchase, a Direct Suggestion is absorbed readily.

- *"I think you've made an excellent choice,"*
- *"In a few days, you'll wonder how you used to manage with your new XYZ!"*
- *"These are so popular at the moment, I'm glad we managed to get yours scheduled for delivery."*
- *"This will keep you going for years."*
- *"This is such great value."*
- *"Things will be so much better for you from now on ..."*
- *"Nice choice. I want one of these."*
- *"This will (allow you to move away from the pain you told me about)."*
- *"This will (allow you to move towards the pleasure you told me about)."*

Development Activity

- *What Convincers sound good to you? What would you feel comfortable saying?*
- *Practise using Convincers!*

Is There Aanything Else
I Can Do for You?

Sales and service are so closely interwoven. Thinking of the sales process as a means of serving your prospective customer is a very healthy attitude and one which will come across in the way you communicate, both verbally and non-verbally.

Asking, *"Is there anything else I can do for you?"* is a great way of reinforcing that message while offering the customer an opportunity to make a last-minute link sale without you even having to ask. Who knows what else the customer has in mind?

Development Activity
- *Whenever the deal is done and the customer has committed, make it a habit to ask, "Is there anything else I can do for you?"*

Business Cards

Offering a business card is a great way of reinforcing that you care – it says, *"You can contact me if you like, I still care about you."* If you're smart, you'll give the customer an extra one or two cards and suggest that you would be delighted to look after his friends or family too. You can make your customer an advocate for you – your very own field sales team!

Development Activity
- *Practise giving out business cards to new customers.*

The Thank You

Saying thank you makes people *feel good*. Remember, so much of professional selling is about how people *feel*.

You can say 'thank you' in number of simple ways:

- At the time of the order – *"**Thank you** for your order Mr Drake, I know you're going to get years of pleasure from your new XXXX."*
- Later, by phone – *"I'm just calling to **thank you** for your order earlier today. I've called the distribution centre and it's all organised for delivery on Tuesday morning as we agreed. OK, thanks again Mrs Griffiths, do let me know if I can help you further, or help your friends, won't you?"*
- By card – a simple **'Thank You'** card posted to your new customer, and hand written, is a personal message that reinforces how important your new customer is to you. You'll be surprised how effective this is.
- By e-mail – not as personal as a hand-written card, but more acceptable these days, as so much communication takes place by e-mail. *"Hi Peter, I just wanted to thank you for placing your order with us earlier today, it's great to have you as one of our new customers. I'm so pleased you chose the XXXX model – I agree this is definitely the right choice for you. Well done! Please do let me know if I can help you or your friends or family. I can always be contacted here at the showroom, or by phone on …"*

Making people *feel good* is a great way to retain customers, gain repeat business and promote your service offer to a wider audience.

Development Activity

- *What 'Thank You' strategies could you develop?*
- *Practise using Thank You strategies!*

The Start of a Long-Term Love Affair

True Professionals are in for the long term. They know that big-ticket selling opportunities will come again with the same customer, or maybe with the customer's friends or relatives.

Keep good records and be prepared to nurture your customers. Smart sales professionals keep in touch and keep the rapport alive. It's a fact that it's easier to sell to an existing customer than it is to start from scratch with a new relationship.

Christmas cards, birthday cards and regular contact with news of promotional events, upcoming deals and new product ranges are all part of keeping a relationship going. You may be surprised how influential a hand-written note, or quick e-mail is in helping a customer 'feel good' about you, your company and your product offers. And let's be honest, there **_are_** times when you're not rushed off your feet, aren't there?

Long-term care creates loyalty. Research shows that customers who are *totally satisfied* are much more loyal, and likely to repeat buy, than those who are only *satisfied*. The True Professional thinks long-term.

Development Activity

- *What are your customer records like?*
- *Do you have a professional customer relationship management system?*

● *What would have to happen for you to set up a system so that you can keep in touch with all those customers who have spent so much money with you?*

'Objections' and Customer Concerns

There are some semantic issues here. Almost all sales training programmes include a section on 'overcoming objections'. Think about the meaning of these words. *Overcoming, objections.*

The phrase *overcoming objections* has connotations of authoritarian dominance and overpowering of customers – hardly a mutually beneficial arrangement built on a friendly relationship and trust. This is really about *Customer Concerns*.

Go back a moment and re-think Customer Concerns. Earlier in the book, we referred to getting inside the customer's world to understand what thought processes are going on. Let's consider two ideas:

1. A Fuller Understanding

In a utopian world, the sales adviser will have conducted such a thorough qualification process that all the buying motives, must-haves, and constraints will have been identified and factored into the demonstration and recommendation stages of the sales process, and customer experience. Everything will have been covered off.

If a Customer Concern exists, it will be because the investigative element of understanding needs has not been rigorous enough, or the customer has been hiding something, in which case rapport has not been deep enough. Customers will only divulge information if rapport has been established and trust developed.

If you have missed a key part in the sales process, go back, re-qualify and start again. You owe it to the customer.

2. 'Feel – Felt – Found'

Sometimes the customer is anxious and is searching around for a subject to be nervous about. Your job is to help him feel less anxious. Using a third party *feel-felt-found* approach is a nice way to help a customer relax.

Feel-felt-found works on the principle that the sales professional understands that the customer is feeling concerned; in fact, recently another customer had expressed a similar concern. Fortunately, when the customer bought the product, he found that his concerns weren't justified.

In other words, *"I know how you **feel**, someone else **felt** the same, but what they **found** was ..."*

"I can understand why you might be concerned about the hotel. One of our regular customers had the same concern when he checked it on the Internet before he flew out last month. He popped in last week and said the building works were all completed. He said it was a lovely place to stay."

"It makes sense to think about wind protection on this bike, especially if you'll be touring Europe on it with your wife. I know that one of our customers, John Jones, tours on his every year. I can remember a similar conversation with him a couple of years ago, before he bought his first 1200

Zakasuki from us. The fairing is just so well-designed in the wind tunnel, it does the job a treat. He's just bought this new model and swears by it."

Or more obviously,

"Yes, I know how you feel. I felt the same before I bought a home cinema system. I wasn't sure if we'd get full use out of it. But what I found was that if you make it a special occasion – we do it once a month – you really get the feel that you're actually in the cinema. It's a wonderful feeling. My husband and children love it – we turn down the lights, turn up the volume and get the popcorn in!"

The True Professional uses *feel-felt-found* with integrity. Make sure you have a genuine tale to tell of feel-felt-found and be proud of the story. Be truthful and honest. Telling genuine stories helps you to come across as genuine and makes you feel more confident. Customers can tell.

3. What Specifically ...?

Sometimes a prospective customer has something bothering her that even she hasn't clearly identified in her mind. We have to help her to find the thing that's bothering her.

"Oh, I don't know, I'll have a think about it at home."

Well, we don't really want her to 'have a think about it at home' do we? Not unless there's a genuine Deadly Delay that really needs attending to. If there isn't a Deadly Delay, there's almost certainly something bugging her that either she hasn't divulged, or that hasn't yet crystallised in her own mind.

We can help by asking a sympathetic question that is kind and gentle.

"No problem at all. Can I just ask what specifically it is you want to think about?"

Notice three elements to this excellent question:

1. There is no pressure on the prospective customer – it's *"No problem at all."*

2. *"Can I just ask ..."* is a polite request to understand – *"just"* is a tentative, mild word that is almost apologetic.

3. *" ... what specifically it is ..."* that the customer wishes to think about.

Notice how gentle the question is. There is no arm twisting or overpowering of the customer. We are simply trying to understand so that we can help. Often this simple 'statement-question' will reveal a customer concern that you really can help resolve. How about:

● Sales Professional
"No problem at all. Can I just ask what specifically it is you want to think about?"

Prospective Customer

"It's just such a step up from my current computer system, I'm not the greatest at computers. I think it might be a bit advanced for me."

"I dunno, I've never paid £900 for a mountain bike before."

"I'm not sure if a necklace is what she wants, or if I should get her a ring?"

"The 1200 cc is a big machine. I don't know if I'm going to be able to handle it when I'm parking it."

"I'm just a bit concerned about the installation. I don't know anyone who can fit it."

"I'm not sure. We've never taken the kids on foreign holiday before. I just wonder if they're too young."

And hey presto! You have a rich pool of information to start working on – all of these 'concerns' are full of useful insights into the mind of the customer – the customer's world – and all of them can be worked on with empathy and warmth. Some of them can be resolved almost straight away, leaving the path clear to once again ask for the order.

Customers, eh? The rotters don't always tell us everything at the Understand Needs stage!

Of course, the *"What specifically ..."* question won't always resolve the customer's concern (whatever if might be). It just gives you a much better chance of doing so. If all else fails, get those details so you can contact the customer in a few days when she's *had a think about it at home* and follow up!

Development Activity

- *Think about possible customer concerns (not 'objections') regarding your big-ticket products.*
- *What genuine feel-felt-found stories can you tell, either third party or your own? Practise using a feel-felt-found when a customer next presents a concern.*
- *Start to think about "What specifically ..." the customer may be concerned about and you'll discover that many concerns can be resolved there and then.*

PART C

taking action

14

knowing what to do is not the same as doing what you know

In the process of learning at work, we know that internal shifts in thinking don't always translate into external shifts in behaviour. Everything you've read so far, no matter how well you've absorbed the material, is of absolutely no use whatsoever unless you use it.

Good old Epictetus had a few thoughts on taking action, too:

> *"And if you are confronted with a hard task or with something pleasant, or with something held in high repute or no repute, remember that the contest is now, and that the Olympic games are now, and that it is no longer possible to delay the match ..."*
>
> *Enchiridion, Epictetus c135 AD*

The True Professional consistently takes massive action using *Meerkat Selling* and consequently gets consistently massive results!

15
principles of achievement

You will only be able to successfully apply the skills and techniques of *Meerkat Selling* if you practise them. There is no rapid route to gaining skill – it requires repetitive use and reviews of performance. What **can** be done quickly is to choose a mind-set that will aid you in your own personal growth; a mind-set of *Commitment*.

As the business speaker George Zalucki says,

> *"Commitment is doing the thing you said you would do long after the mood you said it in has left you!"*

You have to stick to it. *Meerkat Selling* requires practise and a commitment on your part to take time out to reinforce your learning by consciously utilising these techniques in your regular sales activities until you become unconsciously competent. It requires patience and an acceptance that all may not go according to plan at first. You didn't drive the car perfectly on your first attempts, did you?

Learning a new skill can be time consuming in the initial phases of skill development. The fruits of your labour may take a while to grow.

The challenge, as you may know if you have been through a learning process is that the student has to unlearn an established method before the new learning can be installed. This can be frustrating for the learner.

Experienced salespeople are sometimes set in their ways and refuse to change their operating model. This is understandable; many of them have ingrained methods that are unlikely to be shifted easily. Their limiting beliefs prevent them from unlearning their old ways of selling and absorbing a more productive sales process.

If you are prepared to commit to changing your sales beliefs and attitudes and to applying sales behaviours that may be new to you, you will achieve tremendous improvements in your big-ticket selling performance. You may not notice the changes for a while. This is normal. You will begin to notice the mistakes you make, too. This is also normal – it means you are becoming aware of the way you are operating. What's happening is that you are moving through what's called the *Competency Framework*.

16
the
competency
framework

The Competency Framework illustrates the phases we go through when we learn a new skill.

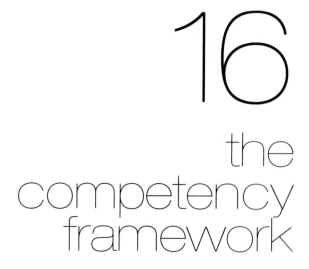

1. Unconsciously Incompetent	4. Unconsciously Competent
2. Consciously Incompetent	3. Consciously Competent

1. When you first started driving with a manual gearbox you didn't even know about *clutch control* – it was a strange phrase that had something to do with driving a car. You were *Unconsciously Incompetent*.

2. Pretty soon you realised how difficult it can be – you were aware that you had become *Consciously Incompetent*. You knew you weren't very good at it!

3. With practise, you began to get the hang of it, and pretty soon you could drive away smoothly by carefully controlling the clutch and maybe even manage a hill start. But it was hard work and you really had to concentrate didn't you? And sometimes you got it wrong and then maybe you felt deflated because you thought you'd already learnt it and yet you were still making mistakes from time to time. You had reached the stage known as *Consciously Competent* – you knew how to do it if you really concentrated.

4. After a while you became a pretty slick driver and you managed to control the clutch without even having to think about it. Maybe you've recently driven somewhere and got out of the car and thought, *"You know, I can't even remember driving here!"* That's when you are *Unconsciously Competent*. You are operating on autopilot!

You've already guessed the Competency Framework connection with the sales skills and techniques proposed in this book, haven't you?

17
'parts' learning

You may be thinking, *"OK, now I understand Meerkat Selling, but there's so much to remember!"*

Fair enough, yes there is a good amount of detail within the 5 Steps and it will take a little practise for you to become unconsciously competent at *Meerkat Selling*. Fortunately, there's a great way to accelerate your learning: it's called 'Parts' learning.

Your challenge is to remember the 'sequence' of *Meerkat Selling* and apply it with your prospective customer.

You're almost certainly a skilled sequence user already. Most people have a set of skills in a given area that involves a sequence of behaviours. They may not be work-related, and that doesn't matter because it's the principle of sequence-skill that is of use to you.

You may be a good cook, a DIY wizard, or a keen gardener. Maybe you enjoy playing a certain sport – golf, cricket, hockey, football, tennis, or squash? Whatever activity you enjoy and in which you have a level of skill, you will already be following a sequence of behaviours that help make you the skilful person you are in that particular activity.

This is important – you are *already* a skilled sequence user. The opportunity for you is to transfer your ability to learn sequence to the learning of the *Meerkat Selling* sequence. This is how 'Parts' learning will help you.

Did you know that different parts of your brain are responsible for different types of activity?

Find a comfortable chair where you're unlikely to be disturbed (and turn off your phone please). You'll only need a few minutes for this. Make yourself comfortable and put your feet flat on the ground with your hands palm down on your thighs. Focus on a point on the wall. Take a comfortable breath and gently exhale, making sure you feel the relaxation as you do so. Now close your eyes (not yet – read and memorise this first!). Once your eyes are closed, continue to enjoy the relaxation and your comfortable breathing. Allow yourself to realise how calming this is becoming.

Relaxation is important, because we don't learn well if we are tense. In fact, anxiety is a learning inhibitor.

Once you are fully relaxed, ask your unconscious mind to find the 'Part' of you that is so good at the activity you enjoy, whether it's golf, cooking, driving, DIY, or whatever is your chosen sequence-skill. This is the *Sequence Part* – the part of you that is good at learning sequences. Now, ask your unconscious mind to find the Part of you that is learning *Meerkat Selling* – the *Meerkat Selling Part*.

Wouldn't it be great if the *Sequence Part* could share with the *Meerkat Selling Part* exactly how it goes about learning sequence? You can do this by simply asking your unconscious mind to introduce the two Parts to each other and leave them to have a chat. Imagine the Parts as characters in your mind. Ask the *Sequence Part* politely, but firmly, to transfer its sequence learning skill to the *Meerkat Selling Part*. How does it learn sequence so well? How did it go about learning the activity you are already good at?

Enjoy a few more minutes of relaxation as the two Parts chat to each other. After a few minutes, you will mysteriously know when **be sure to thank the *Sequence Part* for its help** and begin to 'wake up'. Count from 1 to 10 and open your eyes knowing that you have done good learning work, and that the learning will continue. And you'll notice that you feel great too – a bonus!

And that's it – without you even knowing, your unconscious mind will do the rest as you get on with your daily business. You will be surprised how effective the Parts learning technique is at helping you learn something that you are already really good at – sequence!

It may take time for the learning about sequence to fully transfer to the *Meerkat Selling Part*. Your unconscious mind takes its time to do some things. It takes its own time, and it does it well.

You may have to repeat the process of asking the Parts to talk to each other; in fact I'd encourage you to repeat the process as often as you like – it's a healthy activity.

18

five little dickie birds

Five little dickie birds are sitting on a tree ... two decide to fly away. How many are left? This is a very simple calculation.

Three?

No. Five. Two decided to fly away but they didn't take any action. The same applies to you. Either this book has been an interesting read, or it has been a stimulus for you to take action using the skills you have learned. Which is it? Interest or action?

You can find out more about Nick Drake-Knight at www.ndk-group.com or e-mail to nick@ndk-group.com.

© Nick Drake-Knight 2008

appendix

5-Step Selling Model

Step 1	Meet and Greet
Meerkatting Acknowledge, approach and engage Using your one chance Using your non-verbals Being confident	Building rapport Acting 'as if' Using clean language Using truisms and bridging questions Building trust – what you *don't* need

Step 2	Understand Needs

Understanding the customer's
  Emotional Driver™ (buying motive)
Using good questions
Sharing hallucinations
Getting inside the customer's world
Fuzzy language busting
	Sorting needs versus wants
	Using different strokes for
	  different folks
	Uncovering price expectations
	Discovering constraints and must
	  haves
	Discovering desirables
	Is there anything else?

Step 3	Demonstrate
Understanding features and benefits Fitting with the Emotional Driver™ Feature dumpers and brochure givers Sense selling Test driving	Good, better, best Amplifying customer compliments 'Big up' your finance Avoidance of floppies Yes, and the best way

Step 4	Summarise & Recommend
Fit with the Emotional Driver™ Summarising Yes sets Indirect suggestion techniques Based on what you've told me	Price gaps Finance opportunities Trial closing Link selling Framing and reframing

Step 5	Close
Closing on a first date? ABC Ask for the business Deadly delays	Follow-ups Convincers – the right choice The start of a long-term love affair Objections

Lightning Source UK Ltd.
Milton Keynes UK
UKOW05f0640271213

223628UK00001B/257/P